INTIMATE GLIMPSES OF LIFE IN INDIA

INTIMATE GLIMPSES OF LIFE IN INDIA

A NARRATIVE OF OBSERVATIONS, EDUCATIONAL, SOCIAL, AND RELIGIOUS IN THE WINTER OF 1899-1900

GEORGE TRUMBULL LADD, LL.D.

GYAN

Published by

GYAN

Gyan Publishing House
5, Ansari Road
Daryaganj, New Delhi-110002
Phone: 011-47034999, 9811692060
E-mail: books@gyanbooks.com

Distribution Network
gyanbooks.com
India, USA, Canada, UK, Australia, France

ISBN : 978-81-212-9743-1 (PB)
First Published, 1919

2nd Impression 2023

Printed at: Gyan Press, Delhi.

INTIMATE GLIMPSES OF LIFE IN INDIA
Author: GEORGE TRUMBULL LADD

INTIMATE GLIMPSES OF LIFE IN INDIA

A NARRATIVE OF OBSERVATIONS, EDUCATIONAL, SOCIAL, AND RELIGIOUS IN THE WINTER OF 1899–1900

BY

GEORGE TRUMBULL LADD, LL.D.

Author of "In Korea with Marquis Ito," "Knowledge, Life and Reality," "Rare Days in Japan," etc.

"In this country are born the Buddhas, the Private Buddhas, the Chief Disciples, the Eighty Great Disciples, the Universal Monarch, and other eminent ones, magnates of the warrior caste, of the Brahman caste, and the wealthy householders."

CONTENTS

LIST OF ILLUSTRATIONS

INTIMATE GLIMPSES OF LIFE IN INDIA

INTIMATE GLIMPSES OF LIFE IN INDIA

CHAPTER I

THE INVITATION AND THE JOURNEY

THE winter of 1899-1900 was one of uncommon, though in several respects of extremely painful, interest to the observant traveller in India. The ravages of plague and famine were over extended areas more severe and destructive than ever before under British rule; and the Government was being hampered and even thwarted in its efforts to mitigate the distress of the multitudes, chiefly by their own gross and absurd superstitions. Many of the people believed that the plague had been brought upon the nation through the intercession with the gods of Queen Victoria in her wrath at the defilement of her statue on the *maidan* or public plaza of the city of Bombay. When their relatives were taken away, after their sickness had been concealed until they were in dying condition, to the segregation camps, and of course taken never to return, they credited the rumor that the British had used their blood to prepare cement for the railroad bridges. Inoculation they regarded as the crafty and cruel method of poisoning the surplus population. In the efforts to feed the starving, the usurious native rice merchants were no insignificant obstacle. For they were exporting food, or holding it at high prices for home consumption, while the Government and missionaries were urging, quite properly, that succor should be sent by the shipload from England and America.

To one with insight the political situation was also rendered intensely interesting by the fact that the restlessness and dissatisfaction of many, even of the more educated of the native classes, were being increased by a not very accurate knowledge of the way in which another Oriental people, the Japanese, had forged ahead to a place in the front rank of nations. Why should not India—they were asking themselves—in like manner show herself the equal or the superior of the Western peoples; and so quite capable of governing herself without their assistance, not to say interference? This inquiry seemed more timely and reasonable, and without doubt was more insistent, because just then Great Britain was showing to the world an unexpected weakness and lack of preparation in military matters in its conduct of the war with the Boers.

In educational affairs, too, there were signs of

the ferment of new opinions and new demands everywhere to be detected by the watchful eye, even where they were not made more obvious by being interpreted in the form of confidential conversations. Much of the existing system, in its production of a large surplus of "half-baked" *babus*, who were competing and clamoring for easy government positions, was coming to be regarded as a failure in the more thoughtful native as well as foreign circles. And inasmuch as new ideas were flowing in from abroad, and numerous efforts at reform were breaking forth from the breast of Hinduism itself, and the practices of caste were succumbing to pressure from economic and material changes (for how shall different castes, or those proud of caste and the veriest outcasts, avoid contact when crowded together in a third-class railway car?), opinions and customs on matters of morals and religion were in a most interesting state of transition.

But although the writer had unusual opportunity for gathering impressions in all these fields, lying at that time, as they were, more or less exposed to the eyes of any intelligent and interested observer, the things revealed to him of this sort alone might seem to those who have travelled in India scarcely worthy of being narrated at any such length as to fill a sizeable book. Let it then be frankly—however modestly—affirmed that many of the observations and experiences about to be described are decidedly unusual, and some of them are quite unique. This quality they possess on account of the nature of the invitation which took the writer to India, and of its entirely unexpected and antecedently incalculable sequences.

The story of the invitation to spend the winter lecturing in India—its nature and how it came to be given—needs, then, briefly to be told. Most of this story was wholly unknown to me until after the invitation had been received and accepted; and, indeed, after I had been for some time in the country. The only inkling of any such thing in prospect came in the form of a request from Professor Maher, the celebrated teacher and writer on psychology and philosophy at the Jesuit College in Stonyhurst, England. His letter asked that he should be provided with some favorable notices of my books to send to a friend in India who wished to know more about them with a view to a possible use of them there. With this request my publishers were, of course, entirely willing to comply. I learned afterward that Father Bochum, professor of philosophy in St. Francis Xavier College in Bombay, had refused to teach the courses in this subject required by the Government University, on the ground, as he explained to me, that he and his colleagues came to India in behalf of Christian truth, and could not reconcile it with their mission to inoculate their pupils with what they regarded as the poisonous doctrines of Spencerian agnosticism and infidelity. But this refusal was an embarrassing thing for both the College and the University. For St. Francis Xavier was a favorite college with the Parsees of Bombay; and the Parsees, in comparison with their numbers, were much the most wealthy, well-educated, and public-spirited of the citizens of the Bombay Presidency.

Moved by this conviction, and wishing to get his College out of its embarrassing position, Father Bochum had urged in the committee on curriculum the substitution of some of my books, especially the Physiological Psychology and the Philosophy of Mind, for the works of Mr. Spencer. It should be explained in this connection that the Government Universities in India are not teaching institutions at all. The University sets the curriculum, holds the examinations, grants the degrees, and presides at the greater functions which are held in "Convocation Hall." The affiliated colleges do the teaching, and prepare and present the candidates for the various degrees. And, indeed, this is the only feasible course in India; for you cannot mix Muhammadans, Hindus, Buddhists, Jains, and various Christian sects, not to speak of "agnostics and infidels," in the dormitories, class-rooms and mess of a common college life.

The chairman of the committee on curriculum, who was an Englishman and an avowed disciple of the Spencerian system, did not favor Father Bochum's proposal and demanded to know, "Who is this Professor Ladd; I never heard of him." "So much the worse for you," retorted the doughty churchman, and forthwith wrote a letter to his friend, Professor Maher, begging material that should be of help to his contention. In spite of all, however, my champion was beaten in the committee and his request was denied him. Not at all daunted at this, however, he took an appeal to the University Council or Senate, and there, having the active support of Chief Justice Candy, the Vice-Chancellor, and other influential members, he carried his petition by a two-thirds majority. And, then, on learning that he whose cause he had so pluckily espoused and completely won, was on his way around the world and would visit India, after having lectured in Japan with the *imprimatur* of the Government there, his zeal and courage carried him to unexampled lengths in the resolve to justify and confirm the wisdom of his previous action. With very little dissent in the Senate, and with the yet more active support of the Chancellor, a motion was carried to invite me to lecture in Convocation Hall, under the auspices of the University of Bombay, the first and last lectures of the course being presided over by the Chancellor in person. This action taken was something the like of which had never happened before.

To us, who think so little of established custom, in academical as in other matters, and to whom precedent is of so little account, it is difficult to conceive of the stir which these seeming trivialities made in all India, with reverberations even as far away as Great Britain. One of its principal immediate effects was to make the lecturer suspected of being a Jesuit in disguise. At any rate, I was from the first conspicuously in favor with the Roman Catholics. This, on the other hand, quite regardless of the question whether we stood together for the defence of truth or for the propagation of error, served to "queer" me with some of the Protestant missionaries. My experience, however, is not the only instance which has fallen under my observation, where these good people have seemed to prefer to take sides against those whose competition they most fear in the way of making numbers of converts, rather than with those whose help they ought to welcome in the defence and spread of the fundamental truths of morals and religion. The prestige involved, and the active and not altogether good-natured discussion to which it gave rise in some of the more extreme of the religious press on both sides, in England as well as in India, brought the unconscious and unwilling subject of it all, for the first time in a somewhat checkered life, into the full "lime-light."

The native officials, both high and low, and all

the higher native social classes in India, are prompt and eager to take their cue from the Government circles in their treatment of foreign visitors. This is not altogether due to the very natural desire "to be in the swim," as the saying is, or to curry favor with those in positions of economic and political control. In the case of the more wealthy and intelligent of the natives, such an attitude of deference arises in acknowledgment of the conviction that, with all its mistakes and even crimes in the past, and all its present deficiencies, the security and welfare of the entire continent of India depend quite absolutely on the guidance and guardianship of the British Government in India. In spite of the fact that the vastly improved facility of intercourse between India and the "home-country" has operated to increase the number of English women who "come out" to be with their male friends and relatives, and consequently to decrease the number of illicit connections between British officials and native women, there are not a few instances of sincere respect and affection between the two races. For example, Chief Justice Candy did not hesitate to affirm that he had never sat on the bench with any one for whose legal ability and good judgment he had more respect than his native colleague, Chief Justice Ranade; and Lady Candy was mourning the death by plague of her native steward with as much sincerity as could have been bestowed upon a similar affliction in an English family. It is necessary to bear in mind such influences as these in order to understand the *atmosphere* by which we were surrounded during the winter spent in India.

The stay of about two months in Japan, during which I was engaged in giving lectures before the teachers under the auspices of the Imperial Educational Society, and in the Imperial University, besides numerous addresses of a more general character, was by no means without value in preparation for the more difficult work in India. Not only did it give the lecturer more familiarity with the material, since the principal course in the two countries bore the same title, but also more facility in method when addressing audiences so differently disposed toward the speaker as are those of the Orient. For the Oriental does not readily betray his real attitude, either to the person speaking or to the thing spoken. The listener "keeps his face" to the "saving of the lecturer's face"; but, often enough, to the confusion of the latter's judgment as to the way his words are being taken. It is not beyond possibility for the missionary or other foreign teacher to go on talking for years to an Oriental audience without really knowing how they are taking him or his teachings. A firm grasp on the subject, scanty notes but full information, and the art of quick adaptability to the special occasion or changing temper of his hearers, are indispensable for the best success with an Oriental audience.

Just as we were leaving Japan an incident occurred which threw additional light on the curious and complicated secret relations of native and foreign governments in the Orient. Our ship had stopped two days for the customary coaling at Shimonoseki, and was to sail for Hong Kong at the earliest dawn of the next morning. But late in the evening there were unmistakable signs of something quite unusual about to happen. The harbor police were alert in their watch about the ship; the captain kept going to the ship's side and peering curiously into the shadows below. What this was all about, he did not disclose, until we were out of Japanese waters the following morning. It then became known to us in a confidential way, that the celebrated Chinese leader in the attempt of the Chinese Emperor to institute much needed reforms, the now historically notable Kang Yu-wei, had come aboard and was booked for safe delivery to the British Government at Hong Kong. The wrathful Empress Dowager of China, the "Old Buddha," as Li Hung Chang used to call her, after reducing to submission the young Emperor, and having executed such of Kang Yu-wei's friends and relatives as she could lay her hands upon, had set a large price on their leader's head. But he had fled and had taken refuge in Japan. The Government of Japan, quite reasonably, neither wished to have the reformer assassinated on their territory, nor cared to incur the displeasure of China at harboring in safety one of her political refugees. He was, therefore, quietly turned over to the British Government, which, with fewer scruples, could afford a surer protection to such a criminal patriot. Kang Yu-wei occupied the cabin just opposite to ours; and to it he stuck very close, taking all his meals there,—himself cueless in token of his advanced position in the reform movement, but closely guarded by two trusty, though "pig-tailed," Chinamen in front of the cabin door. I contribute gladly this hitherto unpublished bit of the history of attempts at political reform in China. And to this I add my own strong conviction that China will never reform itself without being in a measure compelled and assisted by foreign influences.

The only other experiences of the voyage to Bombay which have any important bearing on the winter spent in India concern the writer's condition of health. A slight attack of malarial fever had been very much intensified by a successful vaccination on the day before leaving Kobe. This fever had increased so that on every other day the patient was confined to his steamer-chair, without pain, to be sure, but without appetite and with diminishing strength, and much of the time not more than half-conscious of his surroundings. Certainly not a very favorable preparation for a winter's lecturing campaign in the trying climate of India. But the Captain had ordered a special reservation of the store of chickens for his sick passenger. When the Chinese cabin-boy brought the first bowl of the ship-cook's preparation to the cabin, he said with an air of disgust: "Missy! cook no makee good chicky bloth; mollow I make chicky bloth for master." Our "yellow angel," for so we came to call him, was better than his word. For his bowls of broth, rich and steaming, and heavy doses of quinine, and the delightful days and nights spent in the open air, on board ship when sailing in the tropics, so far revived the patient that he was able to put up a good fight against his malady, while the ship was on its way to Colombo, Ceylon. After a short visit there (a brief account of which will be given in connection with our return) three days of sailing on an old-fashioned, but for that very reason most comfortable English ship of the Australian line, with its large and airy cabin, abundance of deck-room, and wholesome fare, although it did not land him "quite fit" as the English are wont to say, did tide him over the shoals of that disaster which is so fatal to many travelers in India and the Far East.

CHAPTER II

BEAUTIFUL BOMBAY

IT was scarcely six of the morning in late November, 1899, when the cabin-boy of the "Chusan" woke us with the announcement that breakfast would be at a quarter before seven. When we went on deck the sun was just rising. It would have been worth a much earlier and more inconvenient arousal to see the queenly city of British India for the first time under such favorable circumstances. The low-lying island, or rather group of islands, now made into a peninsula by various fillings and causeways, above which directly in front of the harbor tower the clustered government buildings and other more scattered lofty structures, with Malabar Hill and its villas and bungalows enshrouded in gardens of palms and other tropical foliage, and all backed by the rugged hills of the mainland which rise to an altitude of from 1000 to 2000 feet, make a picture which easily rivals, if it does not surpass that seen from the harbor of Naples. In the harbor itself the ships of many nations lay anchored, just beginning to stir themselves for the day's work.

But our Captain, who wanted to get to the docks to discharge and take on cargo, was not interested in the lovely spectacle. He was fuming in real English fashion at the nonsense of being kept waiting more than an hour in quarantine, when his ship had arrived, with clean papers from non-infected ports, in plague-infested Bombay. As soon, however, as others besides the health-officers were allowed on board, we were greeted by the messenger who had been sent to welcome us and see to the work of getting our luggage through the customs. This was promptly accomplished at a total expense of six rupees and two annas (just about two dollars) including the small camera. Being landed from the ship's launch at the wharf, we were met by our missionary friend and host, Mr. Edward Hume, and a Catholic priest representing Father Bochum. The latter assured me that the press reports which claimed the plague to be diminishing in Bombay were not truthful. It was increasing; he had already been at the bedside of the dying, that morning.

On arrival at the missionary compound in the native quarter of Byculla, we were treated to a new variation in the ways in which your Oriental friends welcome and dismiss you as their guest. This welcome was not *à la mode* Japanese, but *à la mode* Indian. And the pupils of the school had risen *en masse*, as it were, to make a success of it. Across the gate was stretched the word "Welcome" cut in tissue paper and pasted on a background of white. Festoons of bits of colored paper fluttered from the trees along the driveway; and after driving between rows of children clapping hands, on alighting from the victoria, we were greeted with a song.

All through these dreadful days of famine and plague, the bright spots for as many of the sufferers as was possible—and this was at most, only a tiny percentage of the millions of the people—were in the missionary hospitals and schools. The Government was doing what it well could for the scantiest relief of these millions. But it could not furnish them comfort, and the spirit of song and flowers. As we were expressly told, however, "song and flowers accompany everything in India." In this school, two hundred of the youngest were "famine children," who had been taken from the arms of their mothers or picked up from the roadside where they had been abandoned to die of starvation.

It is not our intention, here or in any of the following pages, to attempt the rôle of cicerone, dragoman, or guide-book. But a few words will perhaps help to make more capable of "visualization" the surrounding material "atmosphere" in which the next few weeks of our winter in India were spent. As has already been indicated, the public buildings of Bombay are from the harbor conspicuously imposing. The same thing is true of them when seen from the streets or from the open public places, in which or near which they are situated. Of these the most impressive is the line of public offices and university buildings which stretches along the esplanade and faces the Back Bay. Their architecture is a mixture of Gothic and Saracenic, and the interior decorations are in teakwood, carved by a native workman in native and therefore Oriental designs. The University Library and University Hall were soon to become of most personal interest. Both of these buildings were largely built by the munificent gifts of wealthy natives; the former by Mr. Premchand Raichand, in memory of his mother Rajabai, and called by her name; the latter by Sir Cowasjee Jehangir, and called by the name of the donor. It was in University or "Convocation" Hall that the lectures were given. But since the structure is 104 feet long and 63 feet high to the apex of the groined ceiling, with an apse separated from the hall by a grand arch, and a gallery eight feet broad around three sides, it is manifestly much better adapted for academic ceremonials than for successful lecturing. The reader, therefore, must not imagine the lecturer as shouting at the top of his voice to two thousand persons, most of them indifferent to what was being said, while a few bend painfully forward in the vain effort to catch an occasional word; but, the rather, quietly discoursing to a few hundreds of exceedingly thoughtful adults, grouped closely around him on the platform or on the rows of benches nearest to the front.

It is not, however, the magnificent buildings, the art galleries, or the museums, but the life and thought of the people, high and low, which most interest me when traveling in foreign lands. This is especially true of the Orient, where all that challenges to attention and the effort at understanding and sympathy appeals much more to the sense of mystery, and fascinates the imagination much more deeply, than anything which Europe can furnish. The street-life of the Orient must be seen to be appreciated; its variety of picturesque structures, animal and human forms, costumes, and strange customs, demand for their fullest effect to enter the mind through the eye. Nowhere else is this more true than on the native streets of Bombay, whose only rivals in these respects are the Straits Settlement cities of Singapore and Penang.

Imagine, then, narrow and tortuous lanes, lined with houses several stories high, many of which have carved fronts and projecting stories supported upon elaborately sculptured corbels, with here and there Muhammadan mosques and various kinds of Hindu temples gaudily painted. Back and forth in these streets flow endless crowds of vehicles and human beings dressed in motley costumes of all colors, or with only a not too generous breech-cloth, or even with nothing at all. They are of all climes and races:—"Arabs from Muscat, Persians from the Gulf, Afghans from the northern frontier, black, shaggy Beluchis, negroes of Zanzibar, islanders from the Maldives and Laccadives, Malagashes, Malays and Chinese, throng and jostle with Parsees in their sloping hats, with Jews, Lascars, fishermen, Rajpoots, Fakirs, Europeans, Sepoys and Sahibs."

The poorer of these natives are housed, whole families of the Oriental size in single rooms, into which neither sunshine nor fresh air can ever come directly, because they are ranged on either side of a hall which runs straight through from front to rear. The only means of discharging garbage and offal is to dump it down into some receptacle from this hall's back door. Since the lower stories of many of these buildings are used for the storage of grain, and the rats which infest this grain are the chief bearers of the plague, it need occasion no wonder that the suppression of this dreadful pestilence was no holiday task for the Government of Bombay. At our first drive through these native quarters, our attention was called to the large number of houses decorated (?) with half-circles and whole circles of red paint. The former meant "case of plague here"; the latter completed the story: "Death by plague here." On a single house more than sixty full circles were to be discerned.

As has already been said, the favorite residence of the wealthy and official classes is Malabar Hill. The hill is terraced to its top, from which may be obtained a view that has without exaggeration been called "one of the finest in the world." On the same ridge is the ladies' "Gymkhana," or meeting-place for athletic sports and games. But overtopping all the hill, and all the beautiful but then sorely stricken city, were the "Towers of Silence," with their inaudible but impressive voice proclaiming the fateful truth that the same end comes to all alike.

Our visit to the "Towers of Silence" was interesting, among other respects, in this one peculiar to the student of the history and doctrine of religious symbolism, ceremonial and myth. We were, of course, treated to the customary sights and explanations—the five *towers* which, however, look more like huge gas-tanks than anything else to which we are accustomed in this country, the "everlasting fire" kept burning through the centuries by being constantly fed with small pieces of sandal-wood, the foul birds perched, expectant, upon the walls and neighboring trees, and the surrounding grove. solemn and beautiful, with its cypresses pointing, as the Parsees themselves say, heavenward. It was duly explained how the bodies were placed, quite naked, on the circular "gridiron" formed by the two walls between the outside one and the central well; how the adult males were placed in the outer series of compartments thus formed, the women in the middle series, and the children in the compartment nearest the well; and how, when at the end of an hour or two the vultures had completed their work, the bare bones were removed by the carriers of the dead, gloved and with tongs, cast into the well, and left to bleach in sun and wind until they become perfectly dry and afterward crumble into dust. All this the professional cicerone, either out of deference to the scientific and practical mind of the Westerner, or because he was himself ignorant of the profound spiritual significance of this way of disposing of the dead, wished us to regard as simply a particularly good and safe sanitary custom. But we knew what the philosophy which underlay the ceremonial, the symbolism clothed in these repulsive facts, really signified. For, the triumph of universal purity, physical and moral, over the nastiness of physical and moral evil, was the ideal of the ancestors in Persia of the Parsees of Bombay. And where should the foulness of human flesh, when deserted by the immortal spirit, while waiting for its resurrection be deposited, that it might not defile the sacred universal elements of fire, water and earth?

We were fortunate in being permitted to remain within the enclosure while the first funeral of the day ascended the flight of steps leading to the "Towers." There were only six persons of the procession, in three pairs, each pair united by a scarf or shawl stretching between them. The first pair were the corpse-bearers, and one of them had, wrapped in white, the body of a child which he bore aloft. This "pairship," too, is symbolical of brotherly union; as a matter of fact, in the well of the towers of silence all classes of the Parsees of Bombay mingle as common dust. Two other pairs of attendants followed; and we saw them all come out of the chapel to get a handful of water for their purification, and heard them within chanting or droning their prayers.

The university lectures were "inaugurated," as the saying is, by a reception given to us by Mr. Tata, a wealthy and benevolent Parsee. With reference to the general character of this gathering, it is enough to quote a few words from a long article in the Bombay "Times of India" for November 30th, 1899.

"The gathering was certainly one of the most interesting which has taken place for a long time in the city. First and foremost education, in the advancement of which Mr. J. N. Tata has himself worked so assiduously, was represented. Then there were representatives of all the professions and of nearly every branch of commerce. It was, too, almost an international assembly, and some of the groups which resulted were, to say the least, remarkable. The rooms were admirably adapted for use on such an occasion, and the large number present" (rather more than 1000) "testified to the immense amount of interest which it had aroused."

Addresses of welcome were given by Vice-Chancellor Candy and Chief Justice Ranade. The former made reference to the peculiar relations existing between India and the University from which the lecturer came, through "the benefactions of Elihu Yale of London, lately Governor of the East India Company's possessions at Madras." Nor did he hesitate to refer to the controversy that had resulted in the Senate of the University of Bombay's acceptance of the proposition, "so ably supported by one of its Fellows," which had, after "due investigation of their merits," placed "the Professor's works among our recognized text-books." More enlightening still to the author were the words of the native Judge of the Supreme Bench of the Bombay Presidency. "When the discussion arose," said Justice Ranade, "in the Senate of the University, whether Psychology should or should not be made a subject of study, the objection was urged that no suitable books were available. Then when Professor Ladd's books were named, one party objected because it was claimed that, if a physiological basis were sought for psychology, it would destroy psychology. The other party claimed that it would only give an additional scientific basis for psychology. The old Indian position is different from both these positions. I have glanced through the Professor's Outlines of Physiological Psychology, and find that he takes a conservative position, and while seeking for a physiological basis, yet he retains a true spiritual psychology." (It is exceedingly interesting to recall in this connection that an entirely similar dispute had been carried on in this country, though some fifteen years earlier.)

Succeeding social functions provided for our entertainment may be dismissed with a few words designed to illustrate several sides of the social life, both native and foreign, in British India. At a dinner given by the Vice-Chancellor the guests were most appropriately selected to represent the different educational interests of the city and the Presidency. Besides the officers from the principal affiliated colleges, Mr. J. J. Tata, the host of the week before, and Sir (and Lady) Jehangir, the son of the man who gave the Convocation Hall, were present. Of the men connected with the University, the St. Francis Xavier Fathers seemed much the brightest and best "up with the times"; the native business men were in matters of general information most worth while to question. Indeed throughout all the Orient I was impressed with the high quality of work in education done by the Jesuit missionaries, and by the rather inferior services of the appointees in the Government educational institutions. Perhaps the point of view of too many of them is illustrated by the question "speered at" a confidential friend by the wife of the President of the Government College. This lady was most anxious to know whether "I was not on a money-making tour." When she was assured that I was travelling at my own charges and as the representative of my university, she seemed much surprised.

The dignified bearing and quiet culture of the best of the Parsees was brought to our notice when we were at Sir Jehangir Petit's for afternoon tea. His house is a palace most beautifully located across the road from the sea. Among the few who had been invited to meet us were one of the St. Xavier Fathers —Sir Jehangir's son is a graduate of this college —and the Protestant missionary to the Muhammadans, Rev. Mr. Davis. The son had prepared a brief outline of Parsee doctrine as he understood it, which, whether a product of the most distinguished scholarship or not, was creditable to his seriousness. So was the small but carefully selected private library which I was shown. Both he and his beautiful young wife were constant attendants upon the lectures on "the philosophy of mind."

Quite different, but in a way not less interesting, was an entertainment given to us in the mission-compound where we were guests. Such an entertainment, I run no great risk in affirming, neither would, nor well could, have been afforded outside of India. It was an exhibition of a native juggler and snake-charmer. The entire body of school children were seated upon mats on the ground—boys on one side and girls on the other—while we and our adult friends occupied chairs at the end of the verandah. The juggler had three assistants, two men and a

THE ENTIRE BODY OF SCHOOL CHILDREN

boy. He had brought an assortment—perhaps it would not be impertinent or destructive to the performer's professional reputation to call it "a job lot"—of snakes, consisting of two cobras, one large and one small, a large mud snake, a water snake, and a small snake of a species not known to any one present. A mongoose was tied to a stake near by. He seemed very restless, as though anticipating a fight with one of the cobras. The exhibition of this form of sport was offered for a not extravagant extra charge; but the spectacle was thought to be altogether too bloody and otherwise objectionable as an entertainment for children, and in celebration of a wedding anniversary. For myself, I must confess I should not have otherwise been unwilling to see it, if for no other reason, as a study in animal craft and courage from the psychological point of view. But Sir Mongoose had a bit of a bag slipped over his wagging head, and thereupon promptly subsided. The snakes were displayed; but the slight teasing given to the cobras did not seem to excite them greatly; and since all the skill in handling is tested by the temper of the snake at the moment, the whole affair was much tamer than what we saw not a few times later. For one can scarcely be several months in India and Ceylon without discovering that a chapter on the subject of snakes in these countries cannot be so brief as the celebrated chapter on snakes in Ireland. But the attitude of the common people toward these reptiles is a sufficient refutation of the silly biological theory devised to explain why *all mankind* find the serpent fearsome and repulsive. For all mankind do not. The feelings of the majority of the primitive races, and of the people most familiar with the serpent species in abundance, are not chiefly feelings of fear and repulsion. The sight of a cobra with head raised aloft and ready to strike does not arouse in one the feeling of "snakiness," but the rather of mysterious and respectful awe (the essence of snake-worship?).

The express regulations and, indeed, the very constitution of the University of Bombay barred from lectures given under the auspices of the University Senate any discussion of religious matters in dispute among the different affiliated colleges. But the topic announced for the course then in progress had been "The Philosophy of Mind." Now the nature of the mind or—to use the term familiar to the old-fashioned psychology—the *soul*, is of no merely speculative interest to the various religions, and even to the rival sects of Brahmans, in British and native India. It was, therefore, possible for the lecturer to treat of matters having the keenest theoretical as well as practical interest to all his audience, without necessarily arousing criticism for having transgressed the limits allowed him by his invitation. An audience so heterogeneous but highly intellectual and keenly appreciative of nice distinctions and subtleties of argument would be difficult to find outside of India. The severity of the plague at the time had made it seem wise not to assemble as yet the undergraduates of the affiliated colleges. The text-books which had been the subject of controversy were set for examination in the M. A. courses. The audiences which gathered were, therefore, chiefly those who had taken, or were preparing to take, these advanced courses; they were, indeed, largely the professional men—lawyers, physicians, teachers in the government and missionary schools, —graduates who were in the government offices or in business, with a sensible number of Parsee and English ladies. There were Brahmans of various castes, Buddhists, Jains, Muhammadans, Jesuit Fathers, Christian missionaries, agnostic Englishmen, and perhaps a sprinkling of scoffers at all forms of philosophic opinion as useless attempts at the solution of insoluble and unimportant problems.

The friends who had risked something in securing the invitation—notably, the Vice-Chancellor and Father Bochum—were obviously somewhat nervous over the success of their scheme. But the audience, from the first, seemed satisfied; it increased by several score at the second lecture; then steadily held its own in numbers and attention to the end. At the close, it gave its "endorsement" in the form of the concluding address of the Vice-Chancellor, which the younger men supplemented in a more demonstrative way,—all of which afforded additional impetus to the plan for opening the doors of approach to other opportunities in Northern and Southern India.

Of excursions from Bombay there was only one which had any particular significance; and this only by way of illustrating the amusing experiences which await the traveller essaying to untie a bunch of red tape in India, especially when the knot is held in native hands. We had received an invitation to visit the caves of Elephanta—Gharapuri, "town of the rock" or "of purification," as the natives call them—in the steam-launch of a friend kindly put at our disposal. But when, after some difficulty we had discovered the proper wharf for embarkation without breach of law, we were informed that we could not leave even for a picnic party on a neighboring island without a regular "health certificate." In vain we invoked common-sense, explained that we could not possibly convey plague to anything but the snakes on this uninhabited island, and offered to be inspected by the officer himself or to inspect one another. It was of no use. But we finally obtained permission to be examined by the health officer at the free anchorage. So away—and much out of our way—we steamed, dragging a small boat after us since the tide was to be low, and sought out a small craft somewhat like an exhausted and abandoned canal boat, moored in the shallow waters amidst a crowd of exceedingly dirty native house-boats. Here was certainly a good place to get plague, if indeed it was the authorized place to be certified as still exempt from it. After a dignified delay the officer on board this disreputable craft gave us the required release. We steamed away disgusted, if not also infected.

A detailed description of the caves of Elephanta may be found in the guide-books; we reserve the narrative of how such remarkable structures look, and what they probably mean, for a subsequent visit to the much more unfrequented but notable and wonderful "caves of Ellora" in the dominions of the Nizam.

It remains now to give some account of more or less confidential interviews which threw light on the less obvious situation in matters political and religious, at that time in India.

When we had been in Bombay about a fortnight I received a call from Justice Ranade accompanied by a young man who seemed to act as a sort of secretary. Justice Ranade was at that time president of the Social Reform Congress, and the most distinguished and influential of the would-be reformers in the Bombay Presidency. At first he seemed disinclined to talk of the political situation or of the plans for improvement formed or contemplated by the Association of which he was the president.

On being courteously questioned, however, to

favor me with his views, Justice Ranade began his reply by questioning me about Japan, and manifested the keenest and most intelligent interest in all that I could tell him about the social and political condition and progress of this Oriental people. Even in his judicial mind, however, no clearcut definite plans existed, as to just how the confessedly needed reforms were to be brought about in India; until, at least, there had been a great improvement in the character for probity, honorable spirit of self-respect and self-dependence, on the part of the educated native population. In these important respects, India was then, and is now, very different from Japan. He urged my presence at the National Congress which was to meet at Lucknow, December 26th-29th. With this invitation other engagements did not permit me to comply.

A subsequent visit from Mr. Malabari was much more fruitful in informing and persuading the mind of the listener. Mr. Malabari was reckoned by all one of the most truly Christian (though not in name) reformers in all India. So profoundly trusted was he that, although he was a very frank and earnest critic of the British Government, it was said that his card would secure a private interview with the Viceroy in preference to almost any other man. Mr. Malabari was a Parsee; but his work had been principally for the political and social welfare of the Hindus. I summarize this most enlightening of all confidential interviews touching such subjects, in the following points.

(1) The worst and most hopeless cause of the social and spiritual degradation of the Hindus is the dreadful estate of their women. They have no respect or confidence on the part of their husbands and sons; they are not fit to become wives and mothers. The chief and most difficult enemy of their intellectual and social elevation is the Brahmans, who keep the women ignorant and degraded, in order that they may maintain their influence over them and through them. The case of the Muhammadans is much better on the whole; this is especially true of the genuine Muhammadans of Northern India. In Bengal the Muhammadan is only a thinly varnished Hindu. In their circles there are many cases of much more of family life and of "spiritual" intercourse between husband and wife. The case of the Hindu in modern India has abundance of historical illustration everywhere in the whole earth. Everywhere it has been the priest and the woman who have been the so-called "conservatives," if combined for good, too often also combined as the enemies of all true progress.

(2) The Parsees are in comparison with their numbers the most influential natives in India. But they are quite worldly and "unspiritual;" in only a few families are the highest relations maintained between husband and wife. As to religion, a few

of the old people are trying to maintain the ancient forms and doctrines which they consider orthodox. In fact, there is now no such thing among them as a pure ancient Zoroastrianism. They seem destined in the world at large to lose their distinctive character and become absorbed in the Jews, Christians, Muhammadans, and Hindus, with whom they have intermingled.

(3) Mr. Malabari expressed a high respect for the Hindu character. They are all—as of the very life-blood and most ancient tradition—practical philosophers, or "brooders" over the problems of reality, life and destiny. This is true of the cooly who earns his few pence by day and lies down in his cloth at night to think. His conclusion runs like this: "Am I poor and miserable? Is death at my door, or already over the threshold? What matters it? This is not my real life. It will soon be over. Why resent or resist it?" Mr. Malabari went so far as to say that he considered the Hindu character as much more akin and genuinely respondent to essential Christianity than is that of the Anglo-Saxon.

(4) As to the British Government in India Mr. Malabari made some most striking observations. Never before have I heard anyone enunciate so clearly the truth to which I have persistently called attention in our own international relations. The conquered or subject lower races which stand in the relations of India to England, as to a superior and

dominant race, always serve as a downward drag. "Today," said he, "not only is India becoming Anglicized, but England is becoming Indianized. The vices of India are penetrating England at home. The many virtues of the English rule in India, and the obvious benefits of it are marred by arrogance of demeanor, and by a certain trickiness and excess of diplomacy where the interests of the Government are thought to be at stake. The higher officials are generally men of capacity and integrity of character. But in the country and hill places, away from easy inspection, many of the English officials lead indecent lives, which greatly discredit Christianity.

In conclusion, Mr. Malabari expressed the opinion, in which not a few Western ethnologists agree, that a final product of really Christian civilization may some day arise out of the mingling of East and West.

From another less lofty and "spiritual" point of view the British Government of India was being criticized severely that winter by the natives. One of the wealthy mill-owners had conducted us through his mills in which cloths of silk were made for Northern India, Burmah, and neighboring regions. These mills employed from eight hundred to nine hundred hands, at average wages of fifteen rupees (about five dollars) a month. Eight rupees will support a family of five in the meanest, most beastly fashion; twelve rupees, in fair condition. Sir Jamsetjee gave a most gloomy account of the business conditions and prospects. Ruin had already met, or was staring in the face, the business men of Bombay. On January next all, or nearly all, the eighty mills of the city would be obliged to shut down and their 80,000 operatives would be out of work. "What," he asked, "with this and plague and famine is coming to this doomed city? Meanwhile all the wealthy, instead of using their resources to meet the emergency, are asked to subscribe to the Transvaal war-fund. There, in South Africa, England is spending £200,000 a day in this most unnecessary war." In view of these and similar criticisms, however just they seemed or really were at the time, it is most significant to note the loyalty of both India and South Africa in the present war.

In the minds of the leaders and of the common people of India religion is most intimately, even inseparably, connected with all social and political affairs. Religion is the gift, the genius of the race. But the dominant religion of Hinduism has been degraded and even made vicious and repulsive by the doctrine and practice of caste. It should be understood that, so far as his religious views, apart from caste, are concerned, the Hindu is the freest of all men within the limits of his churchly communion. He may be any kind of a theist or pantheist, or even an atheist or a Christian, in his beliefs, and remain an orthodox Hindu, if he does not break caste. As has already been said, it is the priests and the women who hold in their hands the keys to the prison-house of caste.

But religious reforms of various kinds and degrees have been mooted and tried in India, through the centuries of its religious history, but especially of late years. For Buddhism and Jainism are both the results of attempts at the reform of Hinduism. He who does not understand something of the religions and religious thoughts and feelings of the people of India, has not taken the first step toward a real *understanding* of anything in India. We must, then, make frequent observations and notes by the way, on this side of belief and life, as we travel together through India.

It was before breakfast one November morning that I received a visit from a man whose "religious conversation" was so entertaining and instructive that an hour's delay at that meal was a most welcome experience. I have seldom talked with anyone whose views on the profounder problems of Theism, revelation, and God's relations to the world, agreed more closely with my own than did those of Professor Bhandarkar of Bombay. But he criticized most frankly, though not bitterly, his own countrymen, who are kept back from receiving the truth from others or discovering it for themselves, chiefly by intellectual indolence,—unwillingness to think for themselves and a preference to follow tradition or any one of their own number who might set himself up for a leader, quite uncritically. Caste, pride, and a feeling of opposition to European dominance in politics and in thought were other influences opposed to progress.

That has happened to the religious reformers in India which is apt to happen to all reformers, religious and otherwise, everywhere. They are continually quarreling among themselves and breaking into subordinate sects. Since, however, the reform movement is much more intelligent and influential in Calcutta than in Bombay, and since in the later place we were brought into closer personal relations with the leaders of reform themselves, anything further on this important subject may well be postponed. The particular theistic reform association about Bombay at that time was called "Parthana Somaj," or "Prayer Church." It comprised some excellent and noble men, but was not making much progress or exercising any considerable influence of any sort.

A nobler band of missionaries does not exist upon the face of the earth than are to be found in British India; and nowhere else are they so cordially welcomed and actively assisted by the Government in power. Exceptions must, of course, be made, like the good old lady in Poona, who, on remarking with a pious demeanor that she was praying for Dr.

Barrows lest he might encourage too much the Viva Kananda party,' and being told in reply, "Dr. Barrows is much obliged, for he needs all your prayers, and he also will be praying for the missionaries of Poona," was speechless with surprise and dissatisfaction at the very thought.

The friends who came to bid us good-bye when we left Bombay by the night train of December 15th, told us that the evening papers reported 200 as the toll exacted that day by the dread reaper. This required that the plague should be, somewhat officially, pronounced "epidemic." But through all that dreadful winter the death-rate rose steadily until on certain days it reached the appalling total of 499. That it never once leaped over the barrier set by that one number, and reached a total of 500, seemed little less than due to some mysterious dictate in the councils of the angry gods.

CHAPTER III

TWO NOTABLE CEREMONIALS

DURING our stay in Bombay we were present at two native ceremonials, one of which had never, and the other rarely or never, been witnessed by foreign eyes. The occasions of these ceremonials were as far apart as are death and marriage. In the one case the celebrants were a rather low caste, but wealthy Brahman; in the other, a Parsee couple. As in most Brahmanical ceremonials, so in this, a slavish but not altogether disinterested deference to the priest was displayed in ways to emphasize the wealth of the layman who could afford thus to control the services of his religious superior. On the contrary, the Parsee wedding-ceremony was so conducted in the public grounds and buildings belonging to the religious community as to illustrate and symbolize the same principle of religious brotherhood which dominates the structure and ceremonies of the Towers of Silence.

The invitation to the "Eleventh Monthly Ceremonial" *in memoriam* of the deceased wife of Mr. Tribhowandas Mungaldas Nathubai came in an exceedingly unexpected and somewhat fortuitous manner. This function was very important in at least two different ways. It was the last and most imposing of a series of such ceremonials; and after its completion only was Mr. Tribhowandas at liberty to marry again. But since this was to be his third venture, it was desirable when permission was obtained, to go through the not unpleasant fiction of being married to a sacred tree! For the third marriage is very unlucky; and the life or death of the bridal tree has nothing to do with the delay of marriage number four, or of any subsequent higher number.

The invitation to the "Death Ceremonial" was given while we were engaged in the work of improving another invitation. We had been urged to visit the temples and burning-ghat of the Kapola Banian caste, of which our proferred escort was the president and principal lay-head in Bombay. This caste is chiefly composed of merchants; but an ancestor of Mr. Tribhowandas had been the principal founder and patron of the temples and their surroundings. It was explained in the carriage on the way that long ago there was a little temple on the spot at which the god Ram arrived when he was perishing with thirst. But he shot an arrow, and where it struck a mighty spring of water came to be. We were shown the spring as historical proof of the miracle; but our skeptical missionary friend insisted that the spring was a cistern, and that the water was rain-water. In the "place of burning," all the bodies are cremated except those of the very young (children under eighteen months, or "until their teeth are cut"), and of the Yogis and very holy men. The children need no "purification by fire," since they have not sinned; and the holy men have already *attained* the purity of soul necessary for entering Nirvana. But their skulls are crushed by a blow on the top, and this suffices to let escape the soul. On being questioned as to the meaning of Nirvana, Mr. Tribhowandas said that his caste generally consider it to be annihilation; but he himself could not subscribe to that, since nothing perishes; all is endless motion. However, on defining himself further, he admitted that individual existence might cease; but so much of God as constituted the soul would have to continue to be.

In this burning-ghat, which is very old now and comparatively disused,—its possession seeming to be in a few of the more wealthy families, and so rather exclusive—there were perhaps twenty-five or thirty tombs and monuments. Some of them are raised to wealthy or distinguished members of the caste, who were not Brahmans or Yogis; but in such cases there are no remains buried beneath. Others of them are tombs of devotees or saints, whose bodies may be buried underneath in a sitting posture. We were gravely informed that these holy men had so lived that they had drawn their souls entirely into their heads; and so, when the blow which crushed their skulls was administered, the whole soul easily escaped upward. The apparatus for cremation was very crude: it consisted of two broad and large andirons and two iron posts about five feet high and two inches in diameter. These posts are erected at the corners of a square. On these andirons a pile of wood is laid and the cremation takes place according to a formula described in a pamphlet which our host had caused to be prepared. He was very careful to have us admire the tomb erected by him to his father, which took the shape of a drinking-trough for the sacred cows.

We were next shown the temples, in all of which there prevailed the unwholesome mixture of magnificence with filth and tawdriness which is so characteristic of Hinduism. Elaborate carved silver doors opened to disclose insignificant and cheap idols within. The idols were worshipped for our benefit without any difficulty; for they stood or sat still and seemed to pay no heed. But to worship the sacred cows properly was not so easy a matter. For to tell the sad truth, the cows did not seem to like to be worshipped. The one cow most amenable to this show of reverence immediately shook off the flowers laid on her head and the holy water poured upon her head, her back, and her four hoofs.

Here we got our first sight close by of the lower

and more disgusting grade of the so-called Yogi. Three of these devotees were encountered seated on the ground just opposite a temple to Shiva. One of them, an old man, was diligently reading a sacred text and did not deign to notice us. But the other two were ready enough to exhibit themselves. Nearly naked, smeared with ashes, with countenances half-way between idiocy and insanity, with matted long and filthy hair, they sat smoking an intoxicating drug. On being questioned as to the genuineness of their locks, with a leer, they shook out the snake-like braids and pulled at them violently to show that they would not come loose.

In several of the temples, or shrines, the *lingam* was being made the object of worship; in one, it was carved profusely with blossoms of flowers, and in another a perpetual tiny stream of water was being poured upon it as a petition to the god of rain. The number of Brahmans thronging the place everywhere was large; but more than half of them were boys who had apparently just been "initiated," as the sacred cord made of twenty-seven strands and thrown over the left shoulder plainly indicated.

On the way home we received two additional invitations, one to allow the owner to exhibit his house that very afternoon; the other to come the following day and witness "the feeding of the Brahmans." On accepting the first of these invitations, we were greeted at the entrance by a daughter of our host, a very pretty girl of sixteen, whom her father had shown his independence by keeping unmarried until so late an age, and who carried herself with as modest yet self-possessed demeanor as would have been shown by a well-trained English girl of the same age. She remained in the immense drawing-room to which we at once ascended, even after the crowd of men belonging to the family had assembled to be introduced. But the *married women* did not appear until after the men had departed; although they, too, came down the stairs and bade us "good night," even shaking hands with me. This distinction between the woman's freedom of behavior with foreign gentlemen and with her own countrymen, is common in the best native social circles throughout India. In his case, Mr. Tribhowandas explained it by saying: "I belong to a very orthodox caste; but I am myself very liberal in my actions."

Mr. Tribhowandas, like Justice Ranade, expressed great admiration for the way in which Japan was making progress as a *nation*, and he bitterly lamented the lack of unity in India, while entertaining the hope of India's sometime becoming a united and independent people.

If nothing especially interesting or informing came of the first of the two invitations given on the way home from the burning-ghat, the same thing cannot be said of that which bade us as onlookers to "the feeding of the Brahmans." For this enabled us to witness an elaborate caste ceremonial which had never before fallen under observation by profane eyes.

On arrival we were at once conducted by a servant to our host, and by our host to the garden. Here about one hundred Brahmans of this caste were assembled, seated in a double row upon the ground, with a considerable number of their women and children seated apart. Most of the men had around their loins the silk cloth which signified that they were purified and ready to feast; but some—presumably the poorer—wore only a cloth of not very clean cotton. The feasting itself was viewed from the windows of the house which overlooked that part of the garden. A son of the host poured water from his hands upon the ground, after which a short *mantra*, called "Sankalpa" or "an auspicious song," was chanted aloud. Each Brahman, before he began to eat, poured a little water and strewed a little rice upon the ground, as an offering to the earth; after which he "fell to" in a manner to show that, with due opportunity offered, he could prove himself no mean "trencher man." The food consisted of fried flour-cakes, pulse soup, rice, several vegetable curries, and sweet-meats. They fed themselves with their (purified?) fingers, and in drinking took pains that the water should be poured into the throat without being contaminated by touching the lips. One elderly Brahman was observed to be eat-ing with the left hand only, the right being covered with a cloth. To eat only in some especially inconvenient fashion—for example, by carrying the hand to the mouth under the leg—is supposed to be especially meritorious.

After witnessing the part of the ceremonial to which alone we had been duly bidden—namely, "the feeding of the Brahmans"—we were asked to return to the drawing-room that we might take leave of our host, who had already left us to greet the Shankarā-chāryā or high-priest of the sect who was to perform the "Death Ceremonial" according to the requirements of the *Capola Bania* caste. On taking Mr. Tribhowandas' hand, I asked, partly in a spirit of experiment, mixed with a certain amount of amused naiveté, and partly with a quite legitimate and sympathetic curiosity, whether we (strangers and heathen) were to remain to any part of the ceremony. The question seemed to occasion no little embarrassment; but after a moment's hesitation, the reply was, that inquiry would be made. I have no information as to how many extra rupees had to be bestowed upon the high-priest to obtain his consent; but when our host returned, to our great gratification and surprise, we were conducted to the place of honor on the right hand of the dais.

It should be explained that, on passing through the drawing-room to reach the window from which the "feeding" was observed, we had been shown the details of arrangement for the religious ceremonial, and had had much of their meaning explained.

The room prepared for the ceremonial was very large for a private house, being not less than forty by eighty feet in size. The great carpet in the center was folded back, so as to give access to the chairs and sofas arranged around the wall on the bare stone-floor; this was explained to be a precaution lest the woolen of the carpet should gather and transmit defilement to the holy men who might happen to come in contact with it. At one end of the room a platform or dais was raised some five inches, and on it were two elegantly carved chairs and a sofa for the spiritual leader of the community. In front of the dais stood a round center-table. On the table was a silver salver, and on the salver small silver bowls containing milk, sugar, carmine pigment for the caste-mark, curds, rice, honey, and shredded saffron. Here also was a silver holder for incense-sticks, with the sacred figure of the elephant, a silver censer, a small font with a ladle, and a bountiful supply of flowers. All these were for the worship of the Shankarā-chāryā.

Before the appearance of the high-priest, the rooms had been filled with the devotees of the caste, —the prominent Hindu males seated on the chairs and sofas ranged against the wall, the Brahmans on the floor, and just opposite us in a group apart, the women and children of the family. Not long after all were seated there was a slight commotion at the door, and the priest appeared with several attendants, one of whom carried a long silver mace in his hand, while another swung a brush of long hair over his sacred head, to warn away the flies. He was a strikingly handsome man of apparently about thirty-five years of age,—shapely in limb and with strong and manly features (evidently of pure Indo-Aryan stock). His cloth was of a light salmon color and his turban of the same color trimmed with gold. He strode rapidly forward across the carpet, instead of avoiding it, although his feet were protected from pollution by wooden geta; and at once seated himself in Turkish fashion upon the sofa. On his left hand stationed themselves the man with the silver mace, the Brahman who was to recite the ritual, and several other attendants. Behind him stood the boy with the brush diligently occupied in keeping off the flies. The space in front of us was courteously kept clear in order that we might the better observe the ceremony.

The "Death Ceremonial" (?) was begun by bringing in a large silver salver which was set down just below the feet of the priest, and on it his sandals, being removed, were carefully and reverently placed. The priest then rested his right foot, now bare, upon the sandal, still keeping his left foot under him. Mr. Tribhowandas squatted on the dais at the right, and the ceremonial began by the Brahman in attendance, who was seated opposite, chanting *mantras*, or sacred verses from the Sanskrit scriptures. Then followed the worship of the priest's right foot, particularly his right toe, with all the honors paid to any divine being among the Hindu divinities. This bodily member was crowned with blossoms of flowers; and over it were poured stores of milk, curds, honey, and water: it was anointed with the *kunku* (carmine-colored pigment); and from time to time it was respectfully wiped with a towel. This worship was performed both by our host and by the priestly attendant, or rather by our host in imitation of the attendant. For although Mr. Tribhowandas had published a pamphlet in his name treating of the whole affair, he did not seem himself to be very familiar with its details in an available practical way. This part of the ceremonial over, however, he had his own forehead anointed with the carmine mark of the caste, and then the same "sealing of the forehead" was offered to such of the faithful as desired to receive it. But it was noticed that an entire sofa full of the lay-brethren declined to be thus decorated.

The next stage of this "Death Ceremonial" was undoubtedly more interesting to many of the spectators, and, it is not unlikely, to the Shankarāchāryā himself. It consisted in the distribution of gifts. About the shoulders of the high-priest was thrown an exquisite camel's-hair shawl, of soft yellow color with dark reddish embroidery; and about the shoulders of the attendant Brahman a shawl of carmine color. Upon a silver plate Mr. Tribhowandas poured out a store of rupees, and was followed in this enforced "collection" by his sons and daughter, until no less than rupees fifty were piled upon the plate. Meanwhile, a largess of ten and a quarter annas was distributed to each of the Brahmans present. The extra quarter-anna was added in order that the gift, being properly some multiple of five, might be in "good measure, pressed down, and running over." Then garlands were thrown around the shoulders of the high-priest, a huge bouquet was placed in his hand; and the man with the silver mace cried with a loud voice: "'Salutation to the Maha-raja; let all the people do him reverence." At which the people gave a shout in response.

It was, however, the concluding part of this amazing ceremonial, which although it was most uninteresting to the faithful present, was of all the most interesting to me. It was the sermon; and this in most religious services that make much of ceremonial, is usually most uninteresting. For "substance of doctrine," as it came to me when translated from Sanskrit into Hindustani and from Hindustani into English, if its substance (as I have no reason to doubt) was faithfully preserved, the claims of this Hindu priest were not radically variant from the claims made by the most rigidly orthodox of every sect of all the religions, in behalf of their own scriptures to be the sole possessors of infallible truth. Before beginning, the preacher sent to ask me on what topic I wished to have him discourse! Surely here was a test of good and ready craftsmanship, to which few of any similar craft would wish to expose themselves. But I was not to be outdone by the inquirer in the graciousness of my reply to the inquiry. "We should all wish him in this important matter to please himself." He then commenced speaking in the most fluent manner, taking for his text a paragraph from the Vedas and then translating the paragraph from its original Sanskrit into Hindustani. After this he spoke in Sanskrit to the initiated only.

The discourse began with praise of the Vedas, the sacred and infallible scriptures of the Hindu religion. The Vedas are the original, sole, and impeccable source of true religion. They point out the way to salvation, and there is no other way than that which they point out. Whoever walks in this way and does as the Vedas instruct him, he has the true religion; he is safe; he will attain Nirvana. But whoever departs from this way, his religion is false, and he will not attain salvation but will surely be punished both in this life and in the life to come. But whereas most men are ignorant and cannot understand the Vedas, and therefore cannot of themselves know the way of salvation, the Brahman knows the way. He gives all his time, his entire life to the study of these things. He is therefore to be believed and obeyed, and his instructions are to be followed in every particular. He who disobeys the voice of the Brahman or refuses to learn of him, and follow in the path as the Brahman directs, he cannot find the way of salvation, but is of necessity blind and ignorant, and miserable in this life and in the life to come.

As to the women, however, their chief duty and the summing-up of religion for them, is to be obedient and faithful to their husbands. (It should be noted that just before the address began, some fifty or more women and children had come in at a side door and had seated themselves upon the carpet, in front and at the side of the women and children belonging to Mr. Tribhowandas' immediate family.)

The discourse closed with a general and impassioned exhortation to abide faithful to their religion, to have confidence in its vast superiority to every other religion, and to show respect and obedience to the Brahmans.

After the Shankarā-chāryā had finished his sermon, he expressed willingness to answer any questions or objections which might be proposed. At this an old man, a *Vaidya* or doctor of divinity, as though by arrangement beforehand, promptly arose, and repeated in Guzarati a part of what his spiritual superior had said. But the old man, as though he had enjoyed (?) an experience which had been spared the younger high-priest, waxed especially earnest and excited, and went into more abundant details, when he came to speak of the place and duties of the women. Not to disobey or cross the husband in any way was the special sacred duty of the woman. As for the child-wife, her duty was to be obedient to her mother-in-law. When the speaker reached the climax of his eloquence on this important practical doctrine, the audience of the faithful broke into applause by clapping their hands.

After this address was over, a young man, a member of the family, arose and thanked all present for their courtesy in attending these funeral ceremonies. Then, to my amazement, he branched off into a quite ill-fitting eulogy of me, who had done the family so much honor by consenting to be among those present. And as our host came up to shake hands and bid us good-bye, he assured us that we had enjoyed, in consideration of his dignity, and at his urgent request, an entirely unique privilege. We will let it stand in that way,—the debit of gratitude being altogether against ourselves.

Some additional light may be thrown on this remarkable ceremony by the two remarks which follow. The Shankarā-chāryā is, as the compound word signifies, a "spiritual leader" of the Shaiva sect.

There are four such guides belonging to this sect in Western India. There are *ācharāyās*, or spiritual leaders, belonging to every Hindu sect. By pre-eminence, one great organizer of the Shaiva sect was formerly called the "great," or Shankarā-chāryā. But now the title is given to spiritual leaders of the first rank in the sect. The appointment is partly hereditary and partly by adoption or selection.

The entire performance as witnessed at the house of Mr. Tribhowandas seemed totally lacking in even the formal expression of the feelings which in Western minds would suggest that it was an appropriate "Death Ceremonial." And indeed, it was not so regarded by those who took the principal part in it. It was, the rather, the formal recognition of the Brahmanical doctrine "The All-One is incarnate in the Brahman; the Brahman is therefore a proper object of divine worship." The way to worship is not spiritual, but purely ceremonial; and he who performs the ceremonial, according to Brahmanical regulations, acquires merit, for the body of the Acharāyā, even his toe, is deity incarnate.

The other equally interesting, though by no means equally unique, ceremony at which we were present during our stay in Bombay, was a Parsee wedding held in the buildings and grounds of the community. The invitation came from Sir Jamsetjee Jejeebhoy, who sent his carriage to take us to the place appointed. The entire "plant"—so to say—was the gift of a wealthy Parsee to the Parsee community, and was made some years ago. It consists of two houses, each with at least one capacious room on the ground floor, a hall for feasting, and considerable open space between the two houses,—all surrounded by a wall.

On entering the yard we found a large company already assembled and seated in chairs in the open air; indeed, the whole yard was nearly filled with invited guests and the members of the community. Among the former were a few Muhammadans and Hindus and one European besides ourselves. With few exceptions, all were dressed in white, which is the proper ceremonial dress or wedding-garment. A band of a dozen or fifteen instruments—mostly brass—stood playing in the space just in front of where the bride and her family friends were waiting for the groom. On inquiry, we were told that all those seated without were the male friends and acquaintances of the groom,—another proof that the business interests of the Parsees are widely extended and are not confined wholly to those of their own class. The ladies of his family were waiting in "the house of the bridegroom;" but right across the avenue between the rows of chairs which had been left open for the procession of these female friends, sat the bridegroom and the officiating high-priest. The groom appeared dressed as were the other Parsees present, except that over his arm

THE HOUSE OF THE BRIDEGROOM

hung a creamy white Chudda shawl with a Persian border; while a similar garment was conspicuously thrown over the shoulder of the high-priest.

Soon after our arrival, the band marched from its station to and through the front entrance into the street, and took up its place opposite the bride's house. The company of the assembled guests followed, leaving the groom and the priest, with the more immediate attendants still standing at their post. We had been, with the greatest politeness, conducted into the house where the ceremony was to be performed and seated in the most favorable place for observing and hearing all.

On entering the house we found it already well filled with girls and women, who were said to be the most immediate friends of the bride. In two corners of the room was a group of five or six hired singers, who chanted in rather melancholy fashion good wishes for the couple and laudations of the virtues of the bride. But we were scarcely seated, when we were invited to go to the door and see a most interesting bit of the ceremonial. This consisted of the reception and consecration of the bride's presents. For to inspect and comment upon these tokens (?) of the family's prosperity and the popularity of the bridal couple is not made the conspicuous thing in this country alone. At a Chinese wedding much of the bridal procession consists of hired attendants bearing aloft the presents, cakes and roast pig and all. The display was more modest in this case. For behind a bevy of a dozen pretty Parsee maidens came two serving women carrying the precious store. While these stood waiting on the upper step just outside the door, the bride's sister came forward with a small silver platter, on which an egg was broken and a handful of rice strewn. This mixture was sprinkled (but only symbolically) over the presents, which were then handed over to the bride.

Water was also sprinkled on the floor, and white chalk was scattered through a sort of stencilled plate over a space of the floor some two and a half feet by one foot in size. A low wooden platform—apparently to prevent the bride from wetting or soiling her white satin slippers—was then placed over this decorated space, upon which the bride took her stand. The formal presentation of the presents was conducted in this way. In her extended palms were laid the choice silks, and over her neck was thrown the string of precious pearls. The cones of sugar covered with paper of gold and garlanded with flowers were left standing on the salver.

Scarcely was this performance finished when we were again summoned to the door to witness the arrival of the bridegroom, who already stood waiting on the step outside. Over him a cocoanut was broken for good luck; and to signify plenty, water and rice were sprinkled over him,—this time actually, though in small quantities. He then, attended by the priest and followed by the assistants, entered the room and seated himself right in front of and facing the bride, the back of whose chair was turned toward us. Two priests held in front of him a wide piece of white silk, which acted as a screen between him and the bride, who was now formally again conducted to her seat. This well signified that the groom "took her without seeing her," or as we should say: "For better or for worse." And now, under the silken screen the hands of the pair were joined by the high-priest, and around the bodies of the two was wound a long scarf of white silk. The "tying of the knot" was further completed by winding cotton cord from a new ball of yarn, seven times around the bodies of both. This "pairing," although the occasion of it was so antipodal, reminded us of that to which we had been witnesses in the procession that was ascending the steps of the Towers of Silence at the time of our visit to the place where the Parsees dispose of the bodies of their departed friends. "Till death us do part;" yes, and even after, if the seven-fold cord is not too easily broken.

Before the screen was removed, the priests chanted in both Sanskrit and Zend prayers for the welfare and unity of the two. Then incense was fired in a large brazen vessel, held just behind and to the left of the groom; and the hired singers broke out into a loud song of well-wishing for the newly married pair.

But the ceremony was by no means over yet. The

occasion must be improved by a sermon of quite half an hour in length. The silken screen was now removed; the bride was seated in the same chair beside the groom and on his left; and the white scarf was moved up on to his right shoulder and allowed to slip down over her right thigh,—as *one* person would wear a scarf of the same kind. Then the priest stationed himself in the full front of the couple and, momently throwing at them a grain or two of rice, chanted first in Zend and then in Sanskrit the moral maxims and exhortations fitted to a newly married pair.

At the end of the sermon, the entire ceremonial was quickly finished with the fatherly blessing of the high-priest. We were then allowed to congratulate the newly married couple in the Western fashion by shaking hands; after which, to our great surprise, we were conducted to the Hall where the wedding feast was spread, and were seated at the bride's table on her right. It would doubtless have been most pleasant and instructive could we have remained to the end of the feast; but another engagement called us away when we had just had time to touch our lips to a glass in honor of the bride's health.

On asking why the entire spoken part of the wedding ceremony was given first in the Zend language —popularly though erroneously supposed to be that of the Avesta, or ancient Parsee scriptures,—and then repeated in Sanskrit, the ancient and sacred language of the Vedas, the Hindu scriptures, I was given this explanation: When the Parsees first came to India, they were allowed to remain only on these conditions: that they should refrain from beef, in deference to the Hindus, from pork, in deference to the Muhammadans; and that they should use both languages, in order to prevent the possibility of intrigue and conspiracy.

The Parsees do not approve of early marriages, as do the Hindus. Unless the male is eighteen and the female sixteen, the marriage is not legal according to their law. But at this very ceremony there was present a little, slender Hindu girl, who could not have been over twelve years of age, but who was obviously within a short time to become a mother. We recalled the statement of Mr. Malabari that, in general, the Hindu women are neither physically nor mentally fit to become wives and mothers.

To the watchful eye there were evidences on this occasion, as on every other where one comes into closer social contact with the one hundred thousand Parsees of India, that they are rapidly becoming Europeanized. Although the grounds and buildings where this marriage was celebrated belong to the community, and can be rented for an entire day for a single rupee and the bare expense of the lighting, the wealthier Parsees prefer being "married at home" to being "married in church." Even in this church ceremony, the use of the ring, the wearing of orange flowers, and other particulars, were European modifications. And that has happened with the Parsees, which always happens under similar conditions; there has arisen a division into a more strictly orthodox and a more liberal and progressive sect. One aged Parsee came up to us after the ceremony was finished and assured us in a grieved voice: "This was not at all the true and ancient Zend ceremony."

Two impressions stamped upon our minds by these notable ceremonials in a somewhat violent way were confirmed and deepened by numerous experiences during that winter in India. Most of the ceremonials, of whatever sort, and whether as practiced by the priests or by the people, are practiced and prized as matters prescribed by custom which it is inconvenient or dangerous to avoid, or through which "merit" may be won and stored, rather than as the sincere and intelligent use of rites and symbolism to express and cultivate genuine religious thought and feeling. In the death ceremonial not a trace of genuine affection for the dead, or of hope of future meeting, or of need for every individual to expect and prepare for the same event, or of faith in the eternal validity of right relations between God and the human soul, was anywhere to be discerned. In the wedding ceremony, although it was celebrated as a sacrament needing priestly assistance and consecration that it might obtain the favor of heaven, and meant to be a true and lasting union of souls, the underlying attitudes, appropriate of mind and heart and will, were not more manifest than they are at many a church-wedding in our own land.

But there is another side to all this, full of significance as to the past, and full of hope as to the future. The common people of India are today more essentially religious than are the people of the United States. These rites and symbols mean essentially this: All human life and all its events—birth, marriage, the begetting and bearing of children, the daily life in the family or before the public, and death and what comes after have *religious* meaning and *religious* value. The divine is never and nowhere, and on no occasion, to be considered as separate from, or a matter of no concern to, the life of man. When the beliefs throw off their superstitions, and the imperious dominance of the priesthood is changed to the helpful spirit of brotherly kindness, and the power of caste is broken, then we believe that the Orient will, mayhap, become again the leader of the world, in the purity and force of its religious fervor.

CHAPTER IV

A MODEL NATIVE CITY

WHEN we awoke the morning after leaving Bombay, we were passing through a region sorely afflicted with famine. The Province of Guzerat is ordinarily "The Garden of India" and its Capital, Ahmedabad, is one of the most flourishing of the ancient native cities. But now, with the exception of inconsiderable sections around the few wells that still yield a scanty supply of water, the land is inconceivably desolate. White dust, a small number of fruitless bushes of cotton, withered cactus hedges, and occasional groups of trees which look as though they were themselves "panting for the water brooks," comprise the landscape that from the car windows meets the eye. Of animal life there are only some lean buffalos, which are being kept alive on what remains of dry stubble and the smaller twigs and leaves of the trees. All the other cattle are dying or already dead. In the fields are famine camps, around which skeletons of men and women are languidly doing a bit of work, or are wandering about in the fields, digging roots for their own food, or gathering stubble for fuel or for feeding the buffalos. The only suggestions of real and vigorous life are the monkeys, which are perched in the barren trees, or sitting stolidly by the track, or gamboling across the fields. Yet the mother monkeys are illustrating one of the two kinds of faith into which Hindu humor of the religious type divides this attitude of mind. For there is "cat-faith" and there is "monkey-faith." In the former, the parent seizes the offspring by the nape of the neck and carries it —*volens aut nolens*—to a place of safety: in the latter kind of faith, the offspring clings around the parent's neck and so escapes the threatened danger. Surely, not only the pious but all the people of Guzerat, need both kinds of faith in the present hour.

We broke our journey for an over Sunday at Ahmedabad, "once the greatest city in India," and said to have been from 1573 to 1600 "the handsomest town in Hindustan, perhaps in the world." In Sir Thomas Roe's time, 1615, we are told: "It is a goodly city, as large as London." We were for our stay, the guests of Dr. and Mrs. Taylor. Since the magnificence of Ahmedabad consists chiefly in the character of its mosques and tombs, built and embellished by its Mogul emperors, and since all this is to be seen in yet more magnificent and well-preserved form, in Agra and Delhi, we shall not dwell upon the wonderful stone carving of Rani Sipris' tomb and mosque, "the gem of Ahmedabad;" or upon the delicate beauty of the elaborate structures in memory of Shah Alam,—who was not, indeed, a political ruler but a religious teacher. [The dome of the tomb had been whitewashed (?) by the enterprising government officer, who appears to go in for "revenue only"; but the Viceroy, on a recent visit, had strongly protested at this æsthetical outrage and had ordered the whitewash removed.]

The chief conquest of our stay in Ahmedabad was some slight insight into the Jain religion, and a particularly intimate view of Hati Singh, which is perhaps the most splendid of the Jain temples in all India. These special favors were procured for us by Mr. Manibai, whose grandfather had founded the temple some fifty years before at a cost of a million and a half rupees, and who seemed to have received instructions from his brother in Bombay to show us every possible attention.

On Sunday morning two brothers who were supposed to be scholars in the tenets of the Jain religion, and in its history, called for the express purpose of answering all the questions which I might wish to ask of them. I cannot vouch for the accuracy of the Sunday-school lesson given to me that morning; since Dr. Taylor, who acted as interpreter had great difficulty in getting from my teachers any clear definition of the terms they were employing; and since almost everything they said has been a matter of endless disputation among the doctors of the various sects into which its creed has broken up. But according to the claim of these student-teachers, Jainism originated before Buddhism; and, indeed, Shakya-Muni was himself at the third remove from the twenty-third Tirthankar, or Saintly founder of Jainism. The Jains, therefore, are true transmitters of the pure Aryan religion. But the Brahmans have corrupted this religion.

The reform which Jainism inaugurated emphasized these three things: (1) Revolt from the rule of the Brahman; for salvation is not necessarily through him; but "as a man soweth, so shall he reap." (2) To abstain from all killing, which—even that of the animals—is forbidden as being murder. But (3) in secular matters, such as marriage, the Jain may resort to the aid of a Brahman.

Positively, the religion of the Jains emphasizes both good understanding and good faith and good works. The word which my teachers used for *faith* really meant "insight" or "vision," and so seemed not to differ materially from good understanding. But they explained it rather as confidence in, and obedience to, the six Tirthankars, or spiritual guides of the community. Besides these, the community has a store of Sarus, or holy men and women, who serve as examples and teachers. The end of it all—as in Brahmanism and Buddhism—is to attain Nirvāna (salvation); but the Way of Salvation is, more especially, to keep the twelve vows, of which the first five are fundamental and constitute the minimum required of every true Jain. They are the Maharratas, or great vows; and to these there is universal agreement. But as to the remaining seven, there is variety of opinion; even my informants differed from some of the books, including one written by a Jain of Guzerat.

During our stay in Ahmedabad this theoretical exposition of the doctrines of Jainism was supplemented by a spectacular exhibition of its ceremonial. Mr. Manibai himself conducted us to the temple of Hati Singh and had the *Asti* or evening wave-offering from the five-flamed lamp performed for our special benefit. Of the temple's architecture two features seemed to me especially beautiful. These were the colonade which surrounds the entire temple-enclosure, and on the exterior walls of which, but opening inwards, are the shrines of the twenty-four Tirthankars; and the several arches over the porches, which seemed veritably to be poured forth upward from the mouths of the elephant-heads that rested on the posts of the porch. Peering through the carved doors in front of the shrines we could see the images of the saints; they were made of different kinds of stone—mostly marble—and their eyes looked as though they were crystals with spectacles over them! Much of the carving of the temple was beautiful and appropriate to a building for religious service; but some of it was as grotesque and inappropriate—for example the Nautch girls dancing—as is much of the carving on the stalls of some of the cathedrals of England.

Just inside the temple door was the shrine of the founder, whose image, resembling that of the Tirthankars and of the god of the temple, and the images of his two wives, appeared behind a screen in the form of a two-leaved door. This particular deity, to which the temple is dedicated, is Dharmanath, the "lord of religion." Before the beginning of the service Dr. Taylor warned us not to be frightened at the noise. The priest then advanced and took up a lamp of peculiar shape with five wicks burning; and at once there began the mingled clanging of a large and rather harsh bell and the rub-a-dub of an enormous drum. The ceremony consisted in waving the lamp in a sort of circular motion, just outside the shrine but in front of the enshrined idol; while the bell and the drum seemed to be engaged in a frenzied effort to drown the low mutterings of the priest and the other four or five worshippers. Part of this ceremony reminded one of the "wave-offering" in the Temple of the Hebrews at Jerusalem.

The Jains—their number reaching nearly a million and a half—are one of the most numerous of the heretical sects in all India. They are largely traders and many of them have acquired considerable wealth. This fact, of course, secures for them influence of a certain kind, but they are, not unnaturally, despised and hated by the leaders of orthodoxy in the different Hindu castes. Their claim to antedate Buddhism is probably false; but when Buddhism had become corrupted and had been largely banished from India by persecution, the simpler and less pronounced revolt against priestly tyranny and the doctrine of salvation by ceremonial came more to the front and appealed to the common people. Their particular boast in the way of practical piety is the strictness with which they regard and practice the commandment: "Thou shalt do no murder." For, in the case of the strictly orthodox Jain, the command protects the insects which get into the food, the musquitos which buzz about the ears, and the moths that flit about the lamp or candle. Thus Mr. Manibai, being orthodox as became the chief patron of the temple, excused himself from acting as our escort, in order that he might get to his home and take his evening meal before twilight. But how do such scruples "jibe with" the duties of religion, now that modern science has evolved its theories of bacteria, micro-organism, etc.? As nearly as possible after the fashion of the Hindus who, not desiring to incur the enmity of the spirits of deceased cobras and their enraged ancestors, have their servants carefully gather up the young snakes in some covered receptable and place them in the compound of the nearest foreigner.

But the observations of this part of our journeying through India were not so much directed to matters of religion as to matters of politics. The next stop was to be at Jaipur (or Jeypore), one of the most interesting and prosperous of all the native cities. The government was chiefly "paternal," in the stricter meaning of the word. And a decidedly paternal government under a native ruler is undoubtedly still most suited to the natives of India; —only, however, if the ruler is an unselfish, wise and good man, and if he and his people can be kept from corrupting foreign influences. But in these days, in India, in the Philippines, or anywhere else where conditions are at all similar, to secure such a ruler and such exemption—ah! that is indeed "the rub."

As we went northward the signs of most extreme famine, and of the barrenness it brings, somewhat diminished. More cattle and goats seemed to be still alive; more green spots were around the wells; fewer skeletons were wandering through the parched fields; and in some fractions of acres a veritable handful of grain was growing.

We tumbled out of our berths to dress and pack up in the dark the next morning. On getting from the train we were handed two letters, one from Col. Jacobs, the "Resident" who represented the oversight of the British Government in that region, and one from our missionary host. The former invited us to dinner, but gave the disappointing information that a disease which had broken out among the elephants would prevent the coveted trip to Mount Amber; the other note apologized for not being able to meet us in person, but put us into excellent hands. We were at once given a breakfast of toast and tea (what in India is called *chota hazri* or "little breakfast") and then taken to the three-roomed tent which had been set up on the compound for our accommodation. This accommodation was highly fortunate, if there is any truth in what the two principal hotels were saying about each other on the printed cards handed to us upon alighting. The experience of most tourists of India will confirm my suspicion that each hotel was telling the truth about the other, but not about itself. I quote a sentence from each, to show that such enterprise is not confined to the United States, but has even reached the northern part of a distant and very differently peopled continent. One testimonial of the KAISER-I-HIND HOTEL read as follows: "On arriving at Jaipur I was driven to Rustom's Family Hotel, but had to leave it owing to its inconvenient surrounding and indifferent cuisine. The Kaiser-i-Hind is a vast improvement on it. The rooms are far cleaner, the feed better and the manager more civil." But the other signed testimonial affirms: "Removed from the Kaiser-i-Hind and stayed at RUSTOM'S with my wife and family for a few days, and have nothing but praise to say of the place—extremely comfortable and clean, and food all that could be desired, a great change to the Kaiser-i-Hind Hotel, the Manager of which was rude and impertinent to me." Between these two complaints we could not choose,—having neither desire nor opportunity to sample either hotel.

The physical lay and surroundings of the native city of Jaipur are so remarkable and so necessary to an understanding of its present political condition and its political history, that some more detailed account of them should be given. The ancient capital Amber, five miles from the more modern capital, the city of Jaipur, gives us the key to an understanding of all this. Amber is situated at the mouth of a rocky mountain gorge, and at the foot of a lovely mountain lake. On all sides except the South, where the modern capital lies in a richly cultivated and extensive plain, Amber is surrounded by rugged hills crowned with forts. At the end of the ridge of hills is the so-called "Tiger Fort," and the side of the ridge turned toward the plain on the South is scarped and made inaccessible from that direction; but behind it, in its nest surrounded by natural and artificial fortifications, with a plentiful supply of living water easy to defend, nestles the ancient capital of this Province. The "old place," begun in 1600 (nothing is really very old in India, compared with the antiquity of Egypt and Babylon or even of Greece and Rome), lies low on the slope of the hill, and is a grand and impressive pile. Its suites of rooms rise one above another, and form vistas opening on striking views. On the higher terrace are the apartments of the Maharaja, which are entered by a gateway covered with mosaics and sculptures, over which is a small pavilion with rarely beautiful latticed windows. In the Treasury, there are fabulous but perhaps not altogether incredible stories of the immense amounts of gold and jewels hoarded up. The beginnings of the native stronghold reach far back in history. Amber is said to be mentioned by Ptolemy.

While the ancient city is largely in ruins, the modern city of Jaipur is flourishing, well-preserved and well-governed, and by no means lacking in features of magnificence quite its own. For the Royal House of Jaipur has been, on the whole, peculiarly favored as respects its native princes, ever since Jai Singh II founded Jaipur in 1728. The Raja of the time when we were there, so far as signs appeared obvious to foreign eyes, seemed a ruler not unworthy to be the descendant of the best of his ancestors. At any rate, not being acquainted with, or empowered to go behind the curtain and see, the real actors, whether in the comedy or the tragedy of government, and so decide how much credit was due to native Rajas and how much to British Residents, we will be content to tell what we saw. And what we say seemed to us important testimony to

A WISE PATERNAL GOVERNMENT

the excellences of a good and wise *paternal government*, administered by the native princes under the friendly and kindly advisement and assistance of the prevalent foreign control.

Our first visit was to the Museum where we received a most cordial welcome from the native chief-attendant in charge. He had read of the lectures in Bombay and was most effusive—native like—in his compliments. On the ground-floor of this building is an interesting and large collection of art-work,—especially of the metal and textile work of India, but almost exclusively modern. In the lecture-room of the Museum, examinations for the Government College were at the time being held. For public instruction has made greater progress in Jaipur than in any other states of Rajputana. The College is affiliated with the University of Calcutta. It was opened in 1844 with only about forty pupils; but at the time of our visit the number had already risen to more than a thousand in daily attendance; and in the quality of its work and its success in preparing its students for the University examinations, it did not need to fear comparison with other institutions of its kind throughout the Empire. From the roof of the building the whole situation of the Maharaja's dominions and the wisdom of his ancestor, Jai Singh II, became plainly visible. For there was the semi-circle of fortified hills which surround the ancient citadel of Amber, with its palaces and treasury, and through the only gap in which an ample supply of excellent water flows from the mountain lake. And there was the fertile plain stretching far away outside the walls of the more modern city of Jaipur, within which the cultivators of those plains could drive their cattle, carry their valuables, and betake themselves for defence in case of attack from their ruler's enemies.

From the Museum we were driven to one of the workshops where such things as the Museum displayed were manufactured and could be purchased to the best advantage. A narrow street under an archway led into an exceedingly dirty court strewn with bricks and piles of stone and other débris. From one corner of the court rose a stone staircase which led to balconies running around the courtyard; and here were tables on which the owner who rejoiced in the name of Zoroaster, and was doubtless a Parsee, displayed his repoussé silver and inlaid metal work, his silk cloths and embroideries. In rooms opening off the court below, boys were at work in the various kinds of industry,—among others, in weaving the woolen carpets (India rugs) the owner was sending to the United States.

But the title to fame as a wise and able ruler which may be claimed by Jai Singh II was not left dependent on his political doings alone; for he was a patron of science and "a royal astronomer" as well. A visit to the palace and palace grounds of the present Raja would not have been half complete, if we had not left the carriage for a nearer and closer inspection of the famous *Jantra* or Observatory, which is the largest of the five built by the aforesaid Jai Singh. This *Jantra* is not under cover, but is an open courtyard in which are the remains of the most curious and fantastic collection of mathematical and astronomical instruments which the world contains. Here are dials, gnomons, quadrants, and other immense structures the intended use of which it is difficult to conjecture—for very likely, the science of this astronomer had a mixture of astrology in it, as was not uncommon everywhere at that time. These instruments include huge structures of stone masonry. But that the collection served, in general, good purposes of a scientific character in the hands of this royal astronomer, is established beyond all dispute by the many wonderfully accurate measurements and calculations which they enabled him to make. The largest of the sun-dials records with accuracy a change of two and a half inches in the movement of the shadow for every minute of the sun's time. And there is little difficulty in dividing that space into sixty parts to mark the single seconds. Indeed, it is of record that by the use of this dial an eclipse of the sun was in the maker's time predicted as accurately as could then be done by the astronomers of Europe.

At Jaipur the provisions for alleviating and preventing the sufferings of the people from both famine and plague were far and away the best which we saw in all India. But some of them were such as only a wise and benevolent *paternal* government, having the confidence and quasi-filial affection of its subjects, could undertake or achieve. Like the king of Egypt in Joseph's time, the Raja had made a huge collection of grain to meet the future wants of the people. But he did not need to store it in granaries, for no rain was to be expected in Northern India in the winter season; and as to thieves, a slight patrol of gendarmes provided against them, if any of the people were so disposed. Long, high piles of bags of grain were stretched through the middle of streets. In this way the people were assured that they need not fear being deceived by the Government, when they were told there should be enough for them to eat and, at least, they need not fear to die of starvation. The same paternal authority fixed the price of this grain, so that the "rice merchants" (a term of bitterness and opprobrium in India and indeed somewhat widely through the entire Orient) should not oppress the poor by putting up the price of food. The Government had also gone through the kindly fiction of saving the cattle from slaughter or death by starvation, by buying them at a fair price, and when the time for the Spring plowing came, these necessities of agricultural industry in India were to be sold back to their former owners, without advance in price and on easy terms of payment. Even in these famine times in Jaipur the revenues will meet the expenses; and large accumulations of gold and jewels are said to be still available in the treasury.

The same superiority was even more manifest in the management of the government hospital and poor-house. These institutions were in every way better than those we had seen at Ahmedabad. There, the poor-house had formerly been a prison. Into its narrow and unsanitary quarters had been gathered 514 famished men, women and children. They were in all stages of starvation. For the well (if any could be counted such) the Government provided the shelter of a roof and twice a day a scanty supply of food. They lay, however, on the ground on mats, wrapped only in such rags as they happened to have, or in a piece of hempen cloth furnished as a cover for their nakedness. At Ahmedabad only the sick had a cot and a blanket furnished them. Eighty-six were counted among the sick. But the hospital at Jaipur was clean, not over-crowded, well-equipped, and at its head was a thoroughly educated native doctor with a sufficient corps of assistants. In the poor-house the food was sufficient and, from the native standpoint, fairly good; and all were furnished with blankets.

In these matters and at such trying times, as always and everywhere, it is the *attitude* of the people toward their Government that chiefly counts. At Ahmedabad, the people would not work to draw the water from the wells through the summer months, when something of their crops could have been saved; and now many of them begged or died of starvation rather than go to the public poor-house, because of their persistent belief that the British Government was enticing them in there in order to murder them and get them out of the way. But at Jaipur, how could his subjects suspect any plot of that character to be hatched against them by their own Raja? And, indeed, the good missionary doctor threatened with his whip the only native who approached the carriage to beg, because he knew the man wanted the money to buy opium from a drugshop near by.

There is an amusing but authentic story connected with the custom of that same drugshop. A dog which had become infatuated with the drug used to station himself at the corner near by and stand on his hind legs to beg for the cash, on receiving which he trotted off to deposit it with the merchant and get its value in a bit of opium.

In this native state the relations between the Government and the Christian missionaries are cordial; and what is more unusual, the relations of the missionaries also with the leaders of Hindu thought. Indeed, from the roof of the Museum there was pointed out the compound belonging to a protestant and reforming Hindu sect, which was at one time very radical and locally influential. Its founder was Dadu, a contemporary of Martin Luther. He is said to have left one hundred and fifty-two disciples, about fifty-two of whom nothing whatever is known. Either the founder or some of his immediate disciples—it is disputed which—left a poem of some 5,000 verses of four lines each, all most carefully rhymed, in which his teachings are given in detail. Dadu rejected the authority of the Brahmans, disbelieved in the efficacy of ritual and sacrifice, derided idols; and was in other respects a most daring heretic and infidel from the point of view of Brahmanical orthodoxy. At about the same time, not only Europe but also India, and not through any means of direct communication but by virtue of the reactions which enforced religious orthodoxy is always sure to bring about, was full of revolt against the dogmas of the prevailing religion and the domination of priestcraft. The heretical poem of Dadu is one of the few, but most interesting, of the survivals of the literature which grew out of this and far earlier revolts in India against the orthodoxy of Brahmanism, outside of the writings of Buddhism and Jainism.

After dining with Col. Jacobs, the Resident, and getting from him the more British, but still highly favorable report of the situation, past and present, in Jaipur, we returned to our tent at 10:30, and finding our traveling servant ensconsed on the mats in one of the flies, and a boy sent by the government to guard us, squatted on his heels before the front door, we went promptly to sleep, with a sense of security, and slept soundly until we were wakened for our early-morning start. This "sense of security" had been maintained in spite of a startling story of the recent experience of one of the missionary ladies whose night-lodging had been prepared similar to our own. She was a new-comer to India and had hitherto been skeptical about snakes as a real danger under such circumstances. But one night, when she was kneeling in nightdress beside her bed, saying her prayers, she was aware of something cold touching one of her naked feet. Her first impulse was to give it a kick, thinking it might be the puppy who was in the room. But she checked herself in time to save her life, with the thought that if it were the puppy, she should hear the sniffing noise he would make. The "thing" crawled slowly up her bare leg until it met the obstacle of her thigh, then turned and slowly crawled down again. The frightened girl then threw herself on her bed, fainted quite away, passed from the fainting fit into a deep sleep, and did not come to consciousness until in the bright light of morning, when she was awakened by the noise of her servant killing the cobra in her bathtub in the fly of the tent.

We had no molestation from any of this kind of terror. But my extraordinary and quite unnecessary precautions against robbers came near ending disastrously. For my address-book, with the letter of credit and other valuables inside it, had been bestowed within the case of the pillow under my head; and we had come off forgetting it. However, a telegram followed by a letter, brought it to us in due time, and not a thing was misplaced or missing. We were then quite sure that our experience of the benefits of a paternal government in native Northern India, when the native Raja is wise and well-disposed, and the British Resident is judicious and kindly, was not purchased at too high a price.

CHAPTER V

RELICS OF MOGUL MAGNIFICENCE

FOR nearly two centuries there flourished in Northern India a succession of remarkably able rulers under the general title of the Mogul Empire. ("Mogul" is the Arabic and Persian form of the word Mongol; but its use is customarily restricted to the Muhammadan rule in India, as it was founded by the invader, Baber, who unlike his equally warlike ancestor, Timur, made up his mind, after having conquered the territory, to settle in the plains of Hindustan and found for himself a new empire by the help of his followers.) This period of its flourishing began under the rule of Akbar, justly called "the Great," who was the contemporary of Queen Elizabeth of England. The man Akbar was not only a great warrior and continued his conquests throughout his lifetime until they extended pretty well throughout all India, but he was also a great statesman and civil administrator. In his latter capacity as a ruler, he so arranged the revenues from the land that, with no greater burdens laid upon the people and taking into account the greater purchasing power of the money of that day, they rivalled those got today from the corresponding area by the British. So much of a religious liberal was this Muhammadan emperor that he put Mussulmans and Hindus on the same basis; is said to have had a wife who was a Christian; and actually undertook to promulgate a new state-religion which should incorporate the more obvious truths of so-called natural theology, and include the truths and practices of all the best religious creeds. Akbar proclaimed himself the prophet and head of this new state-church. Every morning this monarch worshiped the sun before the public, as being the representative of the divine soul which fills the universe; but he allowed himself to be worshipped as divine by the ignorant multitude.

The reigns of Akbar's son, Jehangir, and of Jehangir's son, Shah Jahan, and of his grandson, Aurangzeb—the three reigns extending from 1605 to 1707—cover the period of the greatest magnificence and culminating power of the Mogul Empire, and also the period of the beginning of its decay. Each of these sons rebelled against his father; and after the last of them, Aurangzeb, "none of his successors to the throne was anything higher than a debauchee or a puppet." But how few of all the hereditary dynasties, established by force anywhere in the world during the whole length of its entire history, have remained illustrious and firmly seated during a longer time. And not one of them anywhere has left such glorious remains in one respect at least. The reference is, of course, to the glorious remains of the architecture of the Mogul Empire which was achieved by native and foreign labor, under native and foreign influences, during the reigns of these four of its princes. It was chiefly to rejoice our eyes with the sight of this architecture, rather than to give lectures on philosophical or religious topics, that we visited Delhi and Agra.

Our host in Delhi was the missionary physician, Dr. Crudgington, who had spent some years and made important explorations up the Congo, in West Africa. After breakfast we at once started on our round of sight-seeing and went first to The "Fort" which at the time of the Great Rebellion was the stronghold of the city of Delhi. Within its walls had gathered an immense fanatical population with a garrison of not less than 40,000 soldiers, armed and disciplined by the government against which they had rebelled, with 114 pieces of heavy artillery mounted on the walls, a large magazine of shot, shell, and ammunition, and 60 pieces of field artillery, all of British manufacture, and manned by artillery men drilled and taught by British officers. In those days it was no such easy task as it would now be to reduce speedily such a fortified position. The British hesitated at first about bombarding Delhi, both on account of the difficulty of the job and

THE STRONGHOLD OF THE CITY OF DELHI

also from the fear of the moral influence of failure or long delay; and as well, from other scruples. The walls of the inner city in the vicinity of the Fort are built of small but exceedingly hard brick, and the masonry is so good that they still form a solid rocky rampart of fifteen feet thick.

We were shown over the Fort by a "red-coat" who was fairly intelligent and otherwise a good guide. From the walls we looked down upon the Jamma Musjid, which is reputed to be the largest, as it certainly is the most frequented, mosque in all India; and, indeed, for that matter, in the whole world. After the rebellion the British cleared a broad highway straight from the front of the Fort to one of the sides of the Mosque, in order that, in case of another rebellion, they might command it with the guns, without the risk of injuring the intervening parts of the city or killing its innocent population.

The Mosque at Delhi is certainly well worth the sparing for its own sake and without regard to the disturbance which its destruction would have occasioned throughout the Mussulman world. The purity of the architectural effect is, indeed, somewhat diminished by a rather undiscriminating mixture of red sandstone and white marble. But on the whole its exterior is most imposing. It has three gateways; and it rises, a combination of huge frontispiece, and domes, and four angle towers, and two minarets, upon a lofty basement, the whole giving an effect of great variety, elegance, and size. The gateways are surmounted with galleries, on the roof of which are fifteen smaller marble domes, with spires tipped with gold. Above these are fluted minarets, six in number, which have open arched chambers at the top and are surmounted with gilt pinnacles. Each of the three great gateways is approached by a flight of steps of unrivalled grandeur. Under the Mogul Empire only the Emperor himself could enter by the main gateway; and now, only the Viceroy can enter by this way. It is said that five thousand workmen were employed for six years in its construction. At the Northeast corner is a pavilion in which are said to be placed authentic relics of the Great Prophet himself. Jamma Musjid is the pride, not only of all India, but of the Mussulman world; and if it had perished under what were at the time considered the necessities of war, it is likely that its destruction would have left a sore hard to heal between the conquerors and the conquered.

Our principal interest in the Fort was not to hear the story of the part it played in the Great Rebellion, but to see the exquisite gems of Oriental "culture" that still remain "scattered" here and there among the "bare and ugly British Barracks." Of these gems the two most famous are the Diwan-i-Am or Hall of Public Audience and the Diwan-i-Khas or

Hall of Private Audience. The size of the former of these magnificent structures is, indeed, only one hundred feet by sixty, but it was formerly all plastered with chunam and overlaid with gold. It was in a recess at the back of this Hall that the celebrated Peacock Throne, so mysteriously lost, used once to stand. The "Peacock Throne" was "so called from its having the figures of two peacocks standing behind it, their tails being expanded and the whole so inlaid with sapphires, rubies, emeralds, pearls and other precious stones of appropriate colors as to represent life." The French jeweller, Tavernier, who saw the throne when on a visit to Delhi in 1665, describes its marvels as follows: "It was of the shape of a bed, 6 ft. by 4 ft., supported by four golden feet, 20 to 25 inches high, from the bars above which rose twelve columns to support the canopy. The bars were decorated with crosses of rubies and emeralds, and also with diamonds and pearls. In all there were 108 large rubies on the throne, and 116 emeralds, but many of the latter had flaws. (In this later remark we detect the shrewd eyes of the trained expert.) The twelve columns supporting the canopy were decorated with rows of splendid pearls." Tavernier estimated these to be the most valuable part of the throne, the total value of which was estimated at £6,000,000. But alas! since it was carried off by the Persian invader, although it was for more than a hundred years rumored to be still hoarded in the Treasure House of the Shah, it has now perished from sight, though not vanished in oblivion. But if it had not been the Persians who stole it under the title of booty, it would have been some one else; for this way of acquiring valuables is well enough known both to not very ancient culture, and to still more modern *Kultur*.

The best preserved portions of the Diwan-i-Am foreshow the style of decoration which characterized all the most splendid architecture of the Mogul Empire. These are chiefly its engrailed arches, and the elegance of its chunam work inlaid with precious stones or overlaid with gold. But it is in the interior of the smaller building, the Diwan-i-Khas, that "the art of the Moguls reached the perfection of its jewel-like decoration." On a platform rises a pavilion, both of purest white marble, the roof of which is a flat cone and which is supported on a double row of marble pillars. The inner face of the arches, and the spandrils and pilasters which support them, are covered with a richness of flowers and foliage of the most exquisite designs and delicacy in execution, crusted in green serpentine, blue *lapis lazuli*, and red and blue porphyry. In Persian characters, repeated twice in the panels over the narrow arches at the ends of the middle apartment, beginning from the East on the north side and from the West at the south side, and all in richest decoration, runs the famous inscription: "If a paradise be on the face of the earth, it is this, it is this, it is this." But the builder of this palace was forced to learn, like all the remainder of earth's millions: There is not, and there never has been, any such paradise on the face of the earth. But perhaps there is no nearer approach to the symbolical and apocalyptic representation of a sensuous paradise than that which must have been afforded by the architectural achievements and royal magnificence in living of the Mogul Empire when it was at its prime.

My record of Friday, December 22, 1899, runs as follows: "A great day, for it has taken us over ground occupied by various successive dynasties, conflicting religions, and contending races,—a task in sight-seeing which, according to Keene's Handbook for Visitors, ought to occupy one for not less than two days." But our most interesting and distinctive experience was not in the way of visiting ruined palaces, tombs, and mosques, and—guide-book in hand—laboriously digging out details of history and description, but in the form of what might have been a very serious encounter with a crowd of rascally natives.

We had already climbed up to the top of the first story of the Kutb Minar and had admired the scenery from this elevation, but had refused, on the ground that it was not worth while, to climb the nearly one hundred feet still above our heads. The origin of the Kutb is unknown and it is debated whether it was built by Hindus or their Muhammadan conquerors. At any rate it is a "grand monument" to something or to somebody, and fully bears out its pretensions to be a "tower of victory," "the most perfect tower in the world," one of "the seven architectural wonders of India." It rises in a succession of five stories, each one of which is marked out by corbelled balconies and decorated with bands of inscription, to a height of more than 240 feet. The first three stories are fluted and built of red sandstone, but the upper two stories are faced chiefly with white marble. The shaking which it got by an earthquake in 1803 threw down the cupola and disarranged the battlements and balconies, besides giving somewhat of the appearance of a lilt to the whole structure. But it remains one of the pieces of building best worthy of an admiring visit in all that part of India.

Near the Kutb Minar are the ruins of a magnificent mosque, which stands on the platform of an old Hindu temple, and the courtyard of which is surrounded by a mixture of Buddhist, Jain, and Hindu pillars placed one upon another. The original ornamentation of many of these columns has had its heathenish beauty defaced by the religious fanaticism of the Muhammadan conquerors, who took pains to knock off the heads of the gods carved upon them, and otherwise attempted the removal of all temptations to idol-worship. An Arabic inscrip-

THE MOST PERFECT TOWER IN THE WORLD

tion over the eastern entrance to the courtyard states that the materials were obtained from the demolition of twenty-seven idolatrous temples. Inside the courtyard of the ruined mosque is a relic of ancient manufacture and art, which may fitly tame the boastfulness of the Krupp works at Essen and the furnaces of the U. S. Steel Corporation at Pittsburgh and elsewhere. It is the "Iron Pillar," celebrated for its size and its beauty. This pillar is a solid shaft of wrought iron, more than sixteen inches in diameter and twenty-three feet eight inches in length. An analysis of a bit of this pillar showed that it is pure malleable iron of 7.66 specific gravity. Its own history is in brief deeply cut in the form of a Sanskrit inscription on its western face. It records the fame of a Raja of the olden time, who wished to perpetuate a form of bragging from which his successors in sovereignty, both in the East and in the West, have not recovered up to the present time. "He subdued people . . . and obtained with his own arm an undivided sovereignty on the earth for a long period." He, too, was pious, however, and wished to acknowledge that the gods had something to do with the effectiveness of the energy of "his own arm"; for Raja Dhava was a worshipper of Vishnu, and the pillar was probably surmounted by a figure of that deity. The date of the pillar's erection is put in the third or fourth century A. D. How the workmen managed to handle such a mass of iron is perhaps no harder to imagine than how they handled the stones of nearly seventy feet in length and thirteen or more in height which lie at the foundations of the unfinished temple at Baalbek.

When we descended from the Tower we were besieged by an invitation to visit the "Jumping Well" and see the quasi-vaudeville performance which, for a small fee, would be given there. At first we were reluctant, for there was much more than enough, set down in the guidebook as important, to make an extremely full and tiresome day. But here was something to see which was not ordinarily provided, and which, as the adventure—though it might have resulted quite differently—actually turned out, quite compensated for both money and physical effort. It afforded us a rather unique experience of native craft and cowardice.

The "Jumping Well" was distant a full half-mile away, and since the sand was deep, the sun was hot, and there was no trace of any path, the walk was not an altogether pleasant one. But our guide, who as the event clearly showed, had something more than a merely friendly interest in enticing us thither, kept momently repeating the reassuring assertion that we were now already there. When we did reach the place, the well itself proved worthy of a special visit for a traveler who had never before seen, in its better Oriental form, such a source of perennial joy and safety. The well itself was, I should judge, eight or ten feet in diameter (there were no exact measurements accessible), and was said to be 120 feet in depth. It looked—but probably was not really—as much; and it was lined to the bottom with most excellent solid masonry. On one of its sides was sunk a square pit, of perhaps fifteen or more feet across, also with walls of good stone-work, to about half the depth of the well; and from this pit, to the bottom of which descended a substantial stone staircase, iron doors opened at intervals into the well. This was all designed so that the water could be stored as it rose to various heights; and so that, as it sank to lower depths, the lower doors might be opened in succession, from which the women might let down buckets into the waters below.

On our arrival we found a curious and ill-looking crowd of native men and boys already gathered, doubtless to see how the foreign sahib would stand being fleeced, and to what extent. We were at once escorted to a little raised mound of earth from which we could look over the high curb of masonry and see to the bottom of the well. In one of the doors below, but probably about forty or fifty feet from the surface of the water, stood a naked man. "Look, he will jump," said the master of the jumpers, speaking with the authority and pride of an Arabian "master of the horse." We looked, and he did jump, plump into the water below; and then we turned away. "Look again, and still another will jump," said the manager of the show. Somewhat tardily, yet in time to see that a man did jump, we looked again; and then we turned away in very decided and final manner and with the air of one sated with the daring or mystery of a spectacle provided at so small a fee. To the urgent exhortation to look and see yet others take the "daring" adventure—you cannot call it by any word which smacks of tragedy, for the jumps were made feet foremost; and yet let us say as much—we refused to be witnesses: instead of looking over the curb down the well, we stood erect with our resolve and looked the swindling manager of the show right in the eye. But we did hear two splashes in the water, as though some one may have jumped. (We were afterward told that sometimes, when they are not carefully watched, they expedite matters by throwing large stones instead of themselves down the well.) However all this may have been, in an incredibly short time *four* men, dripping with water and hastily slipping their breechcloths on, stood before us; and for all four the manager began to demand the customary backshish of a half-rupee each. "But I saw only two of them jump, and I will pay for only two." At this a wordy argument began, which became more cool but decided on the one part, and on the other more excited and even threatening. Final-

WALLS OF GOOD STONE WORK

ly, this part of the contest ended with a seemingly final settlement: "Well, then, if you will not give two rupees, give one rupee." A single rupee was then handed to the man who most looked like the one we had first seen jump; and he was instructed to divide it with the other man, whom we could not recognize but who had actually been the second one to have the honor of displaying such fortitude and skill before our eyes.

The implied declaration that this was to be an amicable settlement of the controversy did not correspond to the sequent truth of fact. For at once, the demands for another rupee became more insolent and threatening; and a larger and more ugly crowd was all the while gathering. Our guide had anticipated the situation and had, as a matter of caution for his own hide, or in view of his responsibility to the government for the safety and freedom from insult of his foreign guests, already taken to flight. Not even in the distance was he anywhere to be seen. It was certainly time for matters to be taken firmly into our own hands. The woman was therefore placed in front, and at some distance behind came the man who, as a part of his marriage vows, had promised 'to protect," with an angry crowd of natives close by his side or at his heels. Finally, it seemed necessary to take some more decided measures to solve the problem of escaping actual assault. This may be expected from the natives, only when they are in much superior numbers, and you are alone and unarmed somewhere on the sands or in the jungles of India. I therefore adopted the following strategy (I use the personal pronoun in recounting this rather Quixotic adventure, for I believe it is the only time I have assumed the positively warlike attitude since I was—then a boy—drilling for the Union army). I quickly furled my umbrella, converted it into a club, turned and advanced upon the enemy, brandishing my weapon, looking indescribably fierce, and snarling like a tiger. The effect was instantaneous and highly satisfactory. The whole pack slunk away and let us go unmolested.

This trivial incident is told with some detail because it is so distinctive of the temper of the low-lived native crowd in India, and of the way in which it is necessary and possible to control them. For we were really in some danger; and if certain conditions had been allowed to develop, there would have been no little danger in the situation just described. Indeed, not long afterward, there was published an account of a lady and gentleman among the foreign visitors, who at this same "Jumping Well," and doubtless by this same crowd, had been thrown upon the ground, badly beaten, and robbed of considerable money. The same characteristics may be illustrated on a larger scale by what happened in Bombay not long before our visit to that city. A score of English policemen, with no demonstration of violence on their part, and without making any arrests, kept at bay thousands of riotous natives, highly excited at the efforts of the Government to suppress the plague, in the streets of Byculla. But if a scuffle had taken place, and one of those policemen had been set upon by the mob and forced to the ground, he would speedily have been trampled to death or torn in pieces. Such a mixture of cowardice and cruelty are multitudes of the lower classes in India. On the other hand, the great body of the agricultural classes—and the great body of the people belonging to all classes—are of a gentle and kindly temper; and some of the tribes, especially of Northern India, are as brave and sturdy and faithful warriors as can be found anywhere.

Among the things we saw that day as we returned to the city of Delhi by another route, these two were the most notable: the Tomb of Safdar Jang and the Tomb of Humayun. In the cemetery not far from the former is the burial place of the Poet Khusrau, which, although he died in 1315, is still kept continually crowned with flowers. It was to the latter tomb that Bahadur Shah fled and there concealed himself after the British had stormed Delhi in 1857; and outside of it he and his sons, when they had been forced to surrender, were taken and shot.

Our stay at Delhi was made both interesting and instructive by our intercourse with the missionaries,

—those whom we met being for the most part of the English Baptist Mission. Our host, Dr. Crudgington, was one of those who, under the auspices of this Mission, had made the first ascent of the Congo from the West Coast as far as Stanley Pool. He had many thrilling narratives to tell of his experiences with natives and wild animals. Among them one of the most amusing was an encounter with an African chief who, under pretence of hospitality, was trying to detain the party indefinitely that he might have a favorable opportunity for murdering them and getting possession of their guns and blankets. But the Doctor having ordered all to be ready on a certain early morning, held out his hand in farewell to his murderous host, and looking him straight in the eye, tightened his grip upon the black man's hand until the fellow went down on his knees before him, howling with pain,—thus unconsciously illustrating the psycho-physical truth that, in general, the white races have a stronger "grip," physical and mental, than the black.

To illustrate the benefits of a large mixture of the "paternal" element in dealing with the natives of India, we learned of the same conditions of economic and social injustice prevailing here which we had noticed elsewhere. In the last great famine, that of 1897, thousands of bushels of grain were being stored in the granaries of the native dealers for export to foreign countries, while England and America were sending gifts of food to save the starving in the same region. But it is not in India alone, it is perhaps pre-eminently in our own country, that the ethics of distribution, and not the limit of production, is the greater economic problem.

On our way from Delhi to Agra we had one of several experiences with the extremely unsatisfactory management of the state-railways of India. The first-class car was scarcely fit for a freight car; and although the distance was only 139 miles, it took the entire time from 9 A. M. to 5:30 P. M. to cover it. The chief reason for this is that everything is subject to the needs, and even the caprices, of the officials, civil and military, rather than to any fair extent, to the needs and the comforts of the traveling public.

Of all the places in India, and perhaps in the whole world, for seeing sights of wholly-or-half-departed magnificence in things made by human hands, Agra is the chief. For this reason, and because our visit to Agra had little significance or result other than the seeing of these sights, we may be pardoned for telling what we saw in somewhat more of the guide-book style.

Immediately after our first breakfast, our host, Dr. Valentine, drove us in his cart to Sikandra,—Miss Valentine accompanying us on her wheel. The road is that over which the Moguls used to go to Lahore or Kashmir,—the so-called "Appian Way" of Agra to Lahore. On the road we passed one of the *cos-minar*, or cone-shaped stone pillars, like those the Romans used to set up, which were employed by the Mogul ruler, Jehangir, to mark the path over the plains when as yet no highway had been constructed; and where relays of horses used to be stationed for the better despatch of messages requiring haste. At Sikandra (or Sikandarah) is the tomb of Akbar the Great, which in its present condition was constructed by Jehangir, his son, in 1613 A. D. The gateway leading into the garden which surrounds the Tomb is of red sandstone, inlaid with white marble, and with a splendid scroll, a foot broad, adorning it. Many of the stones which pave the way from the gate to the Tomb are inscribed with the names of the donors; others have cabalistic signs upon them, especially a form of X which was supposed to be effective in guarding against the evil eye.

The architecture of the tomb itself is very peculiar. It is a pyramidal building of four stories; three of them are of red sandstone, and the fourth, where Akbar's cenotaph rests, is of white marble. A massive cloister, broken by high central arches, runs around the lower story. The vaulted ceiling of the vestibule, now faded, was originally elaborately frescoed in gold and blue. A gentle incline leads to the chamber where the great monarch rests. Narrow staircases lead to the fourth and highest platform

THIS MOSQUE MAY BE LIKENED TO A PRECIOUS PEARL

which is surrounded by a cloister of white marble, carved on the outside into lattice-work, every square of which has a different pattern. In the center of the platform is the white cenotaph of Akbar, just over where his body was laid away in the dark vaulted chamber below. On the north side of the cenotaph is inscribed the motto of the sect he founded: "Allahu Akbar," "God is greatest;" and on the south side: "Jalla Jalalahu," "May His glory shine." On the top of a white marble pillar, which stands at the head of the sarcophagus, was—so the story runs—set in gold the celebrated diamond, Koh-i-Nur.

In the afternoon of the same day we visited the Fort and the palaces of Akbar and Jehangir, but such splendors of architecture have been for our purposes sufficiently described in connection with the visit at Delhi. The same thing is not, however, true of the *Moti Musjid* or Pearl Mosque." This structure Fergusson describes as "one of the purest and most elegant buildings of its class anywhere to be found." *The* "purest and most elegant," which we saw in India, I am quite ready to say. The exterior of this mosque is faced with red sandstone, but the interior is covered over with marble, some white, some blue, and some gray-veined. The mosque proper, as it stands within its wonderfully beautiful courtyard, has three aisles of seven bays opening on the courtyard, and is surmounted by three domes. There is a front row of supporting pillars, on the eastern entablature of which an inscription runs the whole length in letters of black marble inlaid into the white. The inscription says that this mosque may be likened to a precious pearl; for no other mosque is lined throughout with marble like this.

If, however, we may compare a tomb with a mosque, the mausoleum erected to the memory of the Persian adventurer, whose daughter married Shah Jehan's son, and who became high treasurer of Jehangir, is for its carved work in marble still more wonderful. The tomb of I'timadu-Daulah is externally all, and internally in part, encased in white marble, and beautifully inlaid with *pietra dura* work. On each side of this square building there are window recesses filled with exquisite lattice-work in marble; in each of the corners there rises an octagonal tower. The side-chambers of the mausoleum are panelled with slabs of inlaid marble; but the upper part of the walls and the ceiling are lined with plaster which is ornamented with paintings of flowers and long-necked vases. In the thickness of the outer walls are two flights of stairs, which ascend to the second story. Here the pattern of the floor is the most suggestive of bold free-hand drawing in inlaid work of anything which we had seen.

But the afternoon of this day was reserved for the first of our two visits to that building, the work of the affection for a woman which has been so almost universally acclaimed as the "most beautiful building in all the world." This is the supreme expression of the praise of the Monguls as builders, that "they designed like Titans and finished like jewellers." The glory of Agra, "the most splendidly poetic building in the world," is the Taj Mahal. But although the Taj has been perhaps more frequently copied and more abundantly described than any other building in the world, it needs perhaps more than any other building to be seen to be appreciated. And this is for three reasons: Like every great and beautiful piece of architecture, it depends for its beauty on its surroundings; its only fitting surroundings are the Oriental atmosphere as it prevails in Northern India; and its beauty is so largely decorative, although it has also the beauty of form and proportion. Let us then at once agree with the writer who says: "It can only be described as a dream in marble." And let us repeat with a qualified approval the words of Lord Roberts: "Neither words nor pencil could give to the most imaginative reader the slightest idea of the all-satisfying beauty and purity of this glorious conception. To those who have not already seen it, I would say, 'Go to India. The Taj alone is well worth the journey' "—all of which is fine enthusiasm for the beautiful in a hardened (?) warrior.

We shall not try either to describe in detail the Taj Mahal, or to narrate any of our dreams before or inside of it; but we shall only state a fact or two about it, of the more obvious sort, and then refer the reader to the illustration or to his memory-picture of the reality. In front of the garden in which, seemingly far away, stands the Taj is a gateway of red sandstone inlaid with white marble and surmounted by twenty-six white marble cupolas. Pass the gateway, and you find yourself in a lovely garden, beds of which are filled with the choicest shrubs and with cypress trees of great size and beauty. Through the center of the garden and for its entire length runs a channel of water, which has no fewer than twenty-three fountains distributed along its course. In front of this channel and at the back of the garden rises a platform, faced with white marble, 313 feet square and 18 feet high, with a white minaret at each corner, 133 feet high. In the center of this platform stands the mausoleum itself. The size of the building is a square of 186 feet, with the corners cut off to the extent of 33½ feet. The principal dome is 58 feet in diameter and 80 feet in height. The dome, which is built of brick, is, however, faced with white marble, so that the entire building appears composed of this material, including the smaller domes which are placed at each of the four corners.

But, as has already been said, besides the standards of beauty of form and material, the Mogul architecture must be especially signalized for its exquisite decoration. It is less conspicuously true that

THEY DESIGNED LIKE TITANS AND FINISHED LIKE JEWELLERS

it was designed by Titans than that it was finished as jewellers finish the most beloved of their works. All the spandrils of the Taj, all the angles and more important details, are inlaid with precious stones. While lacking the simplicity and freedom of Greek decorative art, it has therefore the lavish luxuriousness which is so acceptable to the Oriental taste.

But it is on entering the central chamber, beneath which the bodies of Shah Jehan and Mumtaz-i-Mahal, the best beloved wife, who after bearing him seven children died in child-bed of the eighth, are resting in a vault; and after taking time to gaze upward and around in thoughtful and appropriate mood,—that the chastened appreciation of the beauty of the mausoleum reaches its most calm and finished form. Here, under the center of the central dome, enclosed by a trellis-work screen of white marble, "a *chef d'œuvre* of elegance in Indian art," and seen in the softly illuminated gloom of the distant and half-closed openings which surround them, are the "show tombs" of those whose bodies lie beneath the floor. And he who looks must agree with him who has written: "No words can express the chastened beauty of that central chamber."

By agreement of all who have been able to enjoy the experience, a single visit to the Taj is not enough; and the second visit should, if possible, be taken by moonlight. We could not control the moon, but we were fortunate enough to be able to control our own movements. We therefore went again, this time by ourselves, my wife and I; and escaping the escort of the insistent guides, we took our fill of the architectural beauties of the interior of the Taj Mahal. And to the delights of the eye we added the delights of the ear, which were all the more delightful, because unexpected. For when she sang up into that marble dome, so far away above our heads, there came back such an echo as I have never heard and never expect to hear again. There was no woodenness or metallic harshness in that echo. Only to imagine the purest white marble singing "up aloft" and far away, like a heavenly but inarticulate choir.

It is almost shameful to add any criticism of the architectural perfection of the Taj Mahal, even when seen in the most sympathetic spirit and from the most favorable points of view. But one may agree with Fergusson in complaining of a certain stiffness of outline. And to this I venture, timidly, to add that two details are rather offensive to me. These are: First, that the small projecting pinnacles which continue the small minarets have a somewhat weak and finical look; and, second, that the contrast between the common and rather vulgar inlaid work on the lower part of the exterior and the much more delicate work at the higher levels, is too abrupt. We do not wonder, however, that when Shah Jehan lay dying in his palace across the river, he asked to be carried to the tower-room, so that his last gaze might bridge the Jumna and linger on the Taj Mahal, the tomb of his beloved.

Another of our interesting excursions during our stay in Agra was of a totally different character; but it is worth recording. It was to the Government Jail. Here carpets, which have become somewhat celebrated both in England and in the United States, were being woven. Of the 2,000 prisoners detained here, more than 700 were employed in weaving rugs and blankets, and about 500 in extra-mural work. The system of guards was very interesting. Only three English officers were in charge; but all the guards were natives,—among them a good many Burmese; and all except those who were acting as turnkeys, were convicts. Their reward for faithful work is seven days off on each month's term of imprisonment. One immense carpet was being woven for Queen Victoria as a present from a former teacher in the jail who had become a great "swell" and one of her Majesty's pets. He had taught the Queen-Empress a little Persian, and had been most liberally rewarded, to the disgust—it was freely reported—of the then Prince of Wales and of all the officers in the British-India service. I recalled with approval the plan of employing prisoners in work that may encourage æsthetical talent, and give the mind such uplifting activity and comfort as the exercise of any art may bring; for I had seen the thing better organized and more effective for good in some of the prisons of Japan. The untoward truth was that fully two-thirds of these prisoners are discharged only to come back again; whereas, under the helpful influence of a few benevolent and Christian workers, more than eighty per cent of the convicts discharged from some of the Japanese prisons are permanently reformed. This difference may have been partly due to the fact that here in India there was no prison school, except for the boys, and no religious services of any kind,—the latter omission being made almost imperative by the dreadful curse of caste.

On our long journey from Agra to Calcutta we had our usual "mixed" experience with the management of the railways in India. We arrived at Tundla Junction a little late, but not long after one o'clock A. M. No attention had been paid to our telegram asking for a reservation; and since the platform was crowded with intending passengers for the Punjab mail, the chances for sitting up all night seemed altogether too favorable. When the through train arrived at 3:30 P.M. I discovered that the lady who was the sole occupant of the exclusively reserved "*Damen-coupée*" was getting out; and into this we posted, in spite of official regulations; but on promising not to "give away" the station-master, and to vacate myself at Cawnpore, should any lady passenger appear to claim it, we were both allowed to remain. Since there was meanwhile no more legitimate applicant, I stayed on till Allahabad, where we had a late breakfast. But on coming out with a cup of coffee for the lady companion, who had preferred to stay by the luggage and secure her seat in the car, the trouble began again; for a meddlesome female employee of the R. R. Company had instigated the station-master to do his solemn duty, and had placed him under fear of being disciplined by threatening to inform against him. When, however, the lady flatly refused to be left alone, and her escort as flatly refused to leave her, unless she had the protection of some lady companion, or unless the first-class compartment for which he had paid in Bombay were provided for them both together, that was at once done which could easily have been done without any controversy. A compartment, much better than the one we had occupied thus far, was found, and coolies ordered with all haste to transfer our luggage. The total expense of all this righteous treatment was not large, much less than it would have been in Europe, where, too, such things are extremely likely to happen (*sic*).

All day long we were passing through a comparatively uninteresting country, but with the gratifying sight of increasing improvement as respected the traces of the ravages of famine and plague. Indeed, from Mogul Serai eastward, miles of plain, as far away as the eye could reach in any direction, and level as any of our prairies, were green with "tender croppes;" and although it was mid-winter, the rich foliage of beautiful trees greeted the eye,—made to it more grateful because it had become so wearied and almost tearful with the sight of only stunted and withered bushes and white dust.

On awaking the second morning we found ourselves going through a green and swampy country with a "jungle" not far from either side of roadway, in character better to correspond to the conception I had framed of an Indian jungle than did the so-called jungles in Western India. When we arrived in the station in Howrah, the terminal of the city of Calcutta, only about twenty minutes late, we found our host, Dr. Hector, still waiting for us; and we were forthwith conveyed to his residence, No. 2 Cornwallis Square.

THE GLORY OF AGEA: A DREAM IN MARBLE

CHAPTER VI

GLORIOUS DARJEELING

THE Rāmāyana, that sacred epic which has become the Old Testament of one of the Vishnu sects of the present day, declares of the mountains in Northern India: "As the dew is dried up by the morning sun, so are the sins of mankind dried up at the sight of Himalchal." In less chaste and pious language a modern traveler has written: "When God gave men tongues he never dreamed they would want to talk about the Himalyas; there are consequently no words in the world to do it with." Sated as our minds were with the sight of the most magnificent works of human architectural skill, now lying in pathetic half-ruined and neglected condition, we were ready to turn with the greater eagerness and in a spirit of adoration to a vision of the vaster and more enduring works of God. Therefore, it was determined to spend the week intervening between our arrival in Calcutta and the beginning of the course of lectures there, in a visit to Darjeeling for a view of this most glorious of snow-covered mountain-ranges, or—as the English familiarly call them when seen from this point of view—"The Snows." Nor is the more familiar name inappropriate; for the Sanskrit word, Himachal or Himalaya, signifies "snow-abode" or "snow-mountain." We set out with some anxiety, however, and with the prayer that heaven would at least for a few minutes roll up or blow away the thick enveloping screen of winter clouds; for there have been those, and not a few, who have come thousands of miles and waited weeks for this sublime and purifying vision; but have gone away at last without it.

After a busy over-Sunday, filled quite full with open-air and indoor services, we took the 3:30 P. M. train and started on our fateful journey. As usual, the experiences on the railway were not calculated to conduce to one's comfort or to soothe one's temper. Our servant had gone in ample time to secure the accommodations to which we were entitled by our tickets; but scarcely had we got seated when the compartment was invaded by a troup of "sojer boys" with loads of supplies and abundant courage with which to capture all the occupied but unfortified territory of the car. Of course, according to railway regulations, they had no right there. We capitulated, however, and gave up one side of the compartment with the understanding that we might retain possession of the other. There were other troubles by the way. At one of the junctions we were detained an hour by an accident which had happened in the morning to two of the "goods-trains;" further on, for another hour by a "hot-box;" so that we arrived at the Ferry of the Ganges tired, hungry, and cross.

But the memory of these petty annoyances quickly faded quite away as we crossed the sacred river, just as the sun was slowly setting, on the evening of that New Year's day. The peaceful stream, on whose banks and in whose flood so many millions of human beings have worshipped, bathing and praying, and to which they have sacrificed themselves and their offspring, to us who felt nothing of its summons to fearful deeds and degrading superstitions, was only a solace and a charm. The excellent dinner which was served during the more than an hour of crossing, of ham and capon and plum pudding, over which brandy was poured and then burned so that it might fling its own heat into the open air rather than have it confined to the injury of animal organism, lent to the scenery its ameliorating influences.

Arrived at the other bank of the great river, we took the Northern Bengal Railway, which is only a meter gauge, and by the cheerful connivance of a friendly "guard" secured a compartment for ourselves. Before we lay down without undressing on the not very clean but very hard beds, we had a chance to notice that this part of Bengal seemed well-favored agriculturally and that the inhabitants had an appearance of greater vigor than prevailed among the inhabitants further South.

After a night spent at Siliguri, we rose early, followed the instructions to put on extra-warm clothing, and for the sake of obtaining better views chose an open car, in which to make the ascent of the foothills of the Himalayas. The Himalayan Railway is only a two-foot gauge; its cars are raised only a step above the ground, so that they may "sit tight," as the saying is; each car holds only eight persons, two in a seat facing each other, in each of the compartments into which the car is divided, but only part of the way to its roof. The railway runs beside the highway, which had previously been constructed at enormous cost (in spite of the cheapness of native labor, the expense is said to have reached £6,000 per mile), perpetually crossing and recrossing it, and with it zigzagging up the mountain's side. In the great disaster of the landslide at Darjeeling, in the September previous to our visit, the upper part of this railway had been quite completely wrecked. And as we were soon to discover, it had not yet been completely repaired.

For some miles the Himalayan Railway runs straight away over a well-watered and fertile plain and on a grade so nearly level that one need not suspect mountains to be within a hundred miles. When the real ascent begins, however, the scenery becomes more varied and picturesque. It is mid-winter; it is the most northeastern part of India; and we are going to see the enormously deep and extended snowfield of "The Snows." But 2,500 feet above the sea level, the cocoanut palms are growing; up to more than 4,500 feet, the bananas and the almond trees are in blossom, and lettuce and other green-stuff is being cultivated in the little gardens picked out among the stones on the mountain's side. The views down the ravines thousands of feet below would now be magnificent; but alas! at Kurseong, 5,000 feet above the sea, we run into the clouds and do not come out again until we have reached Darjeeling. Of this station (Kurseong) in the mountains we are told that they who walk out in damp weather must beware of the leeches; and that, although there are no tigers around, there are panthers which sometimes carry off the cattle.

Thousands of natives—from Thibet and from Nepal, Lepchas, Bhoteas, Pahareas, and others—are at work repairing the road. Huge baskets of earth and great stones are carried upon the backs and heads of the women, many of whom are well advanced in pregnancy; while the men are engaged in the work of dressing and laying the stone. In places the sustaining walls rise in terraces for more than a hundred feet from the valley below.

At the terminal of the railway—at present not signaled by any station since the road-bed had not yet been made good quite so far as the Town of Darjeeling—we were met by our host, and proceeded to sort ourselves out, so to say, in preparation for the climb of a mile to his house. A round dozen of sturdy mountain maidens, with features like Esquimaux or Alaskan Indians, fought with us and with one another for the luggage. After we had selected two, beaten off the others, and loaded the luggage on the backs of the successful applicants for this job of porterage, we mounted the lady into the "dandy," in which she was to be borne aloft on the backs of four men. Mr. Brown and I on foot led the cavalcade up the hill. At the Manse we were cordially greeted and led to our bedroom where a fire was smouldering. The bearers of the luggage followed us and were as sturdy in begging for *backshish*, after they had received much more than their dues, as they had been in begging and fighting for the privilege of earning it. Nor until I had forcefully, though gently, turned them out and closed the door behind them, did they disappear, alternately growling and chuckling.

After tea and scones Mr. Brown and I set out for a stroll to the place where the slides occurred that had been a few months before so fatal to one of the missionary schools. The amazing thing seemed, that sane persons should continue to erect buildings in such hazardous places, in view of Darjeeling's past experience with landslides. But as not infrequently happens in such cases, the school having the most obviously perilous situation escaped without loss of life; while the schools that had appeared to be more safely situated were carried down the mountain's side and buried in stone and mud too deep for resurrection. A visit was also paid to "Observatory Hill," where some fine views of cloud effects and of the village of Darjeeling were obtained; but nothing could be seen of the snow-mountains, the whole range of which was thickly shrouded in clouds.

We went to bed that night with minds apprehensive of disappointment on the morrow; for although the stars were out, the prospect was not good for a clear sunrise. On waking early and hurrying to the window, through the lower sash one looked out into thick cloud. But one must look aloft if one wishes to see above the clouds the tops of mountains like Kinchinjanga; and through the window's upper sash the giant's enormous white head and shoulders appeared, showing itself as well as it could in the grey twilight before the risen sun had driven the night's darkness quite away. It was necessary to forego morning tea and do part of one's dressing on the run, in order to reach Observatory Hill before the sun should overtop the horizon of the lower mountains in the East and light up the great Western range. But such limitations of appetite and leisurely toilet were amply rewarded.

And now let us display a few physical facts in order to help the imagination re-create the picture of what we saw on that memorable morning of January 3, 1900. We were standing on a "Hill" more than seven thousand feet above sea level, facing Westward, with our backs to the now just rising sun. On the right the mountain's side fell away in a succession of ravines for thousands of feet, so abruptly that it required no great stretch of imagination to picture ourselves as standing on the edge of one vast precipice and looking down into its depths a full mile below. On the left hand, on the slopes of the Hill and in the cup-shaped valley at its foot, nestled, picturesquely, the village of Darjeeling. In front of us, not far away, was an enormous gulf, the bottom of which appeared smoothly paved with the tops of the clouds colored as though under the moonlight; and up through them broke the crests of mountains that were 15,000 ft. and 16,000 ft. high, and some of them higher still. But these were not "*The* Snows." The range entitled in a special way to be named Himachal, the "snowy," for more than a hundred miles in a line somewhat diagonal and at distances varying from about thirty miles to more than eighty miles, rose on our Western horizon to unparalleled heights, as though determined to support or rival Kinchinjanga, their chief, in its enormous bulk and altitude of more than 28,000 feet. And since it was January, and the snows had descended to their lower seasonable level, there greeted our wondering eyes a hundred miles of such

THE RANGE TO BE NAMED HIMACHAL, THE SNOWY

lofty mountains with a "snow-abode," or "snow-field," having a depth by perpendicular measurement of from 5,000 to more than 15,000 feet.

As we surmounted the crest of the "Hill," and stood panting with the exertion, that happened which we had come thousands of miles cherishing the hope to see happen; the sun tipped its rim over the Eastern hills and covered all this vast "snow-abode" with color of rose.

For twenty minutes more we watched the varied play of rising mists, snowy mountains recovering from their morning blush and turning a dazzling white, and changing cloud-effects; and then a veil was drawn over the whole. We went back, by the same path but by no means so fast as we had come, to drink our morning cup of tea by a hospitable fire. Then once more the heavens smiled and threw off their veil of clouds. Since the mountain could be seen from the manse, but not nearly so grandly fine, another start was made for "Observatory Hill." This time the view was equally grand in its general features, but interrupted with intervals of overspreading cloud, which had the effect of painting the views of the landscape below in terms of chiaroscuro rather than in color of rose. A human element was now added to the interest of the scene. A priest was kneeling before a small shrine on the hill-top, burning incense, tinkling a bell unceasingly with his left hand, and with his right pouring out milk and offering rice,—all the meanwhile intoning verses of prayer. The only words which our native companion and traveling servant could understand were: "Great god, hear me; great god, hear me." But soon a solitary worshipper, a woman, came to hang colored bits of cloth upon the poles and stunted trees around the shrine. As for the priest, he was apparently more concerned to attract our attention than the attention of his god,—in respect of which latter result the ceaselessly tinkling bell was expected to do all needed service. What the poor woman wanted—it might be any one of many things, for doubtless her life was full of unalleviated bitter wants —we had no means of conjecturing, since she did not once speak. Perhaps it was for a man-child to be born of her; or, perhaps, hers was a prayer for daily bread. For her the colored rags were to inform the god, whenever he graciously consented to inspect them. But if one is to worship the Great God, whose are the hills, what place on earth is fitter for the "lifting up of the eyes" to Him, than Observatory Hill, Darjeeling?

There has, indeed, been worship offered to the sun and to the mountains from this same spot for hundreds and perhaps for thousands of years. At present most of the worship here is Buddhistic,—Buddhism being the prevalent religion among the Tibetans. The Lepchas are, however, for the most part devil-worshippers. Among the whole of the native population in this region, by whatever title they are called, or care to call themselves, substantially the same low, vague religious consciousness prevails, which is half superstitious fear, and half a blend of more indefinitely religious emotions. Clear consciousness, and especially definite theological views of any sort, are almost totally lacking among the natives in the mountainous regions of Northeastern India.

Besides the views of the Himalayas there are almost no things worth seeing in Darjeeling and its neighborhood. There is, however, one temple of a distinctly Tibetan type in the village of Bhutia Busti, about a mile from Darjeeling. In the afternoon of the day, therefore, I set out with my native companion to visit this temple and notice, if possible, any variations from the outfit and ceremonies of the low-class Buddhistic temples as I had seen them in many other places. There was some difficulty in finding the place, for the miserable dwellers in the huts of this wretched village seemed grudging in their directions to the right way, while all were clamoring vociferously for annas as a fee for acting as our guides. Finally, however, we reached the spot over a muddy and filth-bestrewn path, and were nonchalantly informed that we could not see the inside for less than eight annas. Several ugly-looking and dirty Lhamas were loafing about, and other of the lay brethren of the Bhutias were currying horses just outside the temple. As we came in front of the structure, one of the priests offered to set the prayer-wheels a-going for the regulation price. When I had him informed that I had seen much better temples for two annas, he no more seemed to appreciate my attempt at a jest than did the acolyte guide who, in the crypt of the Coptic Church in Cairo, was showing me where Joseph and Mary sat at the time of their flight into Egypt, when I asked him why husband and wife sat so far apart; but he was equally eager for the *backshish,* and promptly reduced the fee to the two annas. In the lack of any intelligent guide who could speak English, and in view of the dangerously filthy look of the interior of the temple, and the fierce aspect of the men in whose escort we should be confined, we came away content with having looked through the window upon the gods and their shrines of Bhutia Busti.

There is another point of view from which "The Snows" can be seen to great advantage, that was easily accessible from the Manse where we were staying. This is Jalapahar, the hill where is now situated the British cantonment for invalided soldiers. The cantonment had been earlier built at great expense on Mount Sinchal, 8,400 feet above sea level; but after three years' occupancy it was abandoned because so many of the officers and soldiers committed suicide on account of overpowering loneliness.

On the second day of our stay, therefore, we rose early and, in spite of the prevailing thick clouds, climbed Jalapahar in the hope of seeing another sunrise on the Himalayas. There were beautiful but restricted views to be obtained by the way. But when we had reached the top and had followed the path through the grounds of the cantonment to the extreme edge of the cliff on which it stands,—clouds and mist having suddenly been swept away,—the effect was so unexpected and surprising that I burst into a shout and clapped my hands for joy. We were now standing 8,000 feet above sea level, and looking off on snowy mountains, the highest of which towered more than 20,000 feet above the point of view. A veil of mist covered them, as nearly as the inexpert eye could essay to measure such a thing, to the height of about 14,000 feet. The vale below us and the nearer and lower heights were seen with all that beauty of cloud effects,—fleeting lights and hurrying shadows,—of which only such mountains are capable; while across the higher altitudes of the mountains themselves the fleecier clouds were drawing slowly in changing and fantastic shapes or lingering lovingly around them. We had speechless, because inexpressible enjoyment for a full half-hour of this sort; and we then came down to spend the rest of the day writing letters and shivering with the cold.

The next morning was set for our starting back to

Calcutta where the lecturing was to begin on the following Monday. But we were going to walk along the heights and sides of Jalapahar to the station at Ghoom, four miles from the Manse; and there was hope of getting other grand views of "The Snows" from several points on the way. This hope became courage when, just as we were about to rise, there was a rap on the bedroom door, and the voice of our host called out cheerily: "The Snows are visible and will be clearer soon." From the front of the Manse we saw the Himalayas once more rose-colored with the rising sun; but within a brief half hour the clouds gathered around them again. This was as though they were jealous of their proud beauty, lest too long or too frequent display of it should render it common for mortal eyes.

With two coolies carrying the luggage, and Mr. Brown walking with us and acting as guide, while his *syce* led the horse on which he expected to ride back, we set out for Ghoom. Various glimpses and fuller views of the mountains, all varying in particulars or in the type of their characteristic beauty, were allowed us by the way; and after we had taken one last, fond lingering look at Himachal we came down to the iron bands of the railway, so suggestive of human achievements and human misdoings, if not with our sins dried up, as "the dew in the morning sun," at least with memories which will greaten and lift up the spirit until all memories forever fail.

Besides the reward of so many of the grandest sights which nature can afford, we had picked up many facts about the natives and their relations to the Government, that shed some light, in however half-comical a way, upon the difficulties which beset the more familiar relations of the two. The children of these mountain regions swarm and seem much more hardy and better fed, in spite of any law of Malthus, than are the children in the plains below. But here, as everywhere, the curse of the peasants is the money-lender and the rice-merchant. It is not uncommon for the poor, when they have to borrow in order to get seed or to save themselves from starvation, to be charged seventy-five per cent compound interest. I was told of one crofter, who in a time of drought had run in debt for 10½ rupees (about $4.50) worth of rice. Five years later he had paid on the loan 76 rupees, and still owed 140 rupees. Surely *monts de pieté* under the jurisdiction of the Government would be a decided godsend to the poor in many parts of India.

But some means would have to be devised to protect the dependents themselves from becoming ultimately the chief sufferers from the help rendered to them too freely. For nowhere in the world is the general principle that injudicious and excessive help from others weakens or destroys the desire and the power of self-help, more flagrantly illustrated than among the natives of India,—especially, perhaps, the natives of Bengal. Of all types of men rendered worthy of pity, but incapable of winning respect, there is, so far as my experience has gone, scarcely another so conspicuous as are a moiety of the Bengalese *babus*. Now the word "babu," it should be understood, is properly a polite form of addressing a Hindu gentleman, corresponding fairly well to our "Sir" or Mr.; but it has come to be disparagingly used of a Bengal youth who, having received a part of a university education, or only having made a "try" at some of the examinations, affects the manners of an Englishman, expects to be regarded as a preferred candidate for some petty government position, and thus to secure a larger dowry from the father of the girl whom he condescends to marry. But surely, we should get down from the mountains to the lower and more sordid things of life in India, before we pursue this subject further.

On the journey down to Siliguri, although there was always much cloud, we had opportunity to marvel at the magnitude of the work done in the construction of the Darjeeling-Himalaya Railway, and to wonder at the grandeur and beauty of the scenery which is visible from its tracks. And when, toward sunset we came in sight of the plain of all North-eastern India lying some 2,000 feet below; its green and greyish fields, and river courses, and pools, shining like a mosaic of gold and silver, stretching away, and stretching upward, until they united with the sky in one limitless Turneresque picture, and all flooded and blended with the glory of the light of the setting sun; we were content to return, refreshed and purified by intercourse with nature, to ordinary intercourse with mortal and sinful man.

Arrived at Siliguri, we found that a letter from our kind and thoughtful host at Darjeeling had secured us a sleeping compartment. At sunrise we were crossing the Ganges, and after a really hot bath—the first in six days—and tiffin in Calcutta, established the habit of looking back on the trip to Darjeeling with an absolutely perfect satisfaction.

CHAPTER VII

THE CAPITAL CITY

IN its situation and external aspects the City of Calcutta does not compare at all favorably, either for its beauty or its interesting sights, with the City of Bombay. Instead of being surrounded on three sides by the sea and backed by imposing hills, it lies straggling along a dirty river, at an elevation of only about twenty feet above tidewater. Like Bombay, it has a large commerce with which are concerned ships from all parts of the world; but its port is too thin and ragged to be impressive.

Moreover, the Hugli is a very difficult and dangerous stream to navigate, not only on account of the cyclones, in some of which a storm-wave has overwhelmed thousands of people living along the banks, but also because its shoals are so constantly changing that only a daily experience of the changes can enable the pilot to take his ship safely to its dock. The Hugli cannot be navigated at all at night, and in the daytime only when it is at flood tide. Nor are the buildings and public places of Calcutta as fine as those of Bombay. The same thing is true of its principal streets, whether used for business or for residence purposes.

Perhaps a more important difference is due to the inferiority in enterprise and social development of the native inhabitants of Calcutta. There are almost no Parsees here,—the race which we found to be so wealthy and influential in the rival city of Western India. Although there are now several hundred thousand Muhammadans resident in Calcutta, this class have never had such control of affairs here, where the comparatively modern enterprise of the English East India Company planted itself, as to leave any impress upon its architecture comparable to, or even resembling, that of Delhi and Agra. Of the Hindu natives the great majority are Bengalis; and of the Bengalis, by no means the uniformly best have gathered into its capital city.

At the time of our visit Calcutta was the capital city, not only of the Bengal Presidency but also of the entire British Government in India. Since then, in 1905, the Province has been divided, in spite of much dissatisfaction and display of rebellious spirit on the part of its people. The reason assigned for the partition was its unwieldy character. However valid, or invalid, this reason may have been, the uncertain and turbulent nature of the Bengalis, as they were even at that late day in this capital city, may be better understood if we emphasize the following picture of the populations controlled from the beginning under the British Government of the Province of Bengal. "The people," we are informed, "exhibit every stage of progress, and every type of human enlightenment and superstition, from the educated classes to primitive hill-tribes. On the same bench of a Calcutta college sit youths trained up in the strictest theism; others indoctrinated in the mysteries of the Hindu trinity and pantheon; with representatives of every link in the chain of superstition—from the harmless offering of flowers before the family god to the cruel rites of Kali, whose altars in the most civilized districts of Bengal, as lately as the famine of 1866, were stained with human blood."

There were two subjects, however,—and these in importance inferior to *no* others,—in which the weeks spent in Calcutta were superior to *all* others, with respect to the information they imparted and the insight which they tended to stimulate. These were the effects, including both benefits and deficiencies, of the British system of educating the natives of India; and the successes and failures of the various efforts of the native leaders at social and religious reform. The thoroughness and detail of the investigation in these two directions which I was able to make were very much increased by the facts that there was then in Calcutta no prevalence of plague or famine to interfere with the smooth running of the educational institutions; and that the

Brahmo-Somaj were holding their annual meetings and were therefore greatly in evidence; that we were being entertained, in the most familiar and friendly way, in the families of two of the leading missionary colleges; that Mr. Kali Banurji, a thoroughly educated lawyer, the most influential and universally respected and beloved of all the converts from Hinduism, gave almost his entire time to being our guide and instructor; and that the leaders of the Brahmo-Somaj, and the heads of the various educational and religious institutions, and even the Viceroy himself, showed us the very extremes of frankness and courtesy.

Before we speak of these more important matters, however, a few words about the lectures—the audiences which attended them and the reception which they met—will not be without instruction bearing on what is to follow. They were given in the evening, in a large hall, on the "Philosophy of Religion," and under the auspices, more particularly, of the missionary colleges. These missionary colleges are "aided," however, by the Government, and are considered an integral part of the Calcutta University. At the beginning of the first lecture the hall was crowded; but several hundred of those present were boys who showed that their only motive for coming was curiosity, by getting up and leaving the room, one by one or in groups of half-a-dozen or more. However, the audience that stayed by until the introductions, lecture, and concluding remarks were over, numbered five hundred or more. It was necessary to learn and practice composure in the sight of such fickleness; but this it was not particularly difficult to do as soon as it became apparent that the custom was prevalent among the Bengalis of the student classes, and meant no particular disrespect to any particular speaker. The lesson was afterward of considerable use in addressing Korean audiences, who, in this as in some other regards, resemble those of Bengal. Besides, the attraction to make an early exit was often increased by the fact that nearly opposite the hall where the lectures were given the meetings of the Brahmo-Somaj people were being held nightly; and that they had adopted the measures of the Salvation Army for drumming up an audience by heading the procession with a noisy band of instruments of brass and instruments of percussion. These are not favorable to placidity of philosophical discussion. However, the faithful part of the audience did not diminish, but they rather increased; there was always on the platform, as a sort of body-guard, some of the most distinguished of the educated Hindus and native and foreign Christians; and in the body of the house several hundred of attentive, if not highly intelligent, listeners. The fact of chief importance, however, was this: it was *Religion* which was being discussed; and with the majority of those present, religion was the subject of chief intellectual and practical interest. When, toward the close of the course a special meeting was arranged for the purpose, the questions proposed were pertinent and well-expressed. They comprised such topics as "The Arguments for the Being of God," "The Eternity of God and His Relations to Space and Time," "The Reconciliation of the Divine Omnipotence with Man's Individuality," and other themes of a lofty speculative character, such as would scarcely be brought forward by college students in this country.

After the last lecture of the course, a Dr. Sarkar, who was the only native then living that had received the degree of LL.D. from Calcutta University, and who had a great reputation as a writer on "science," and a Justice Banurji, who was much admired as a high-caste orthodox Hindu, because he himself reported that, while his mother lived, he daily drank the water in which she washed her feet, both made congratulatory remarks. Then a printed testimonial was read and presented by a Philosophical Club in the Assembly's College, and another by a representative of the Presidency College; there was a "response" and an exchange of handshaking and farewells; and this part of the work of the winter in India was at an end.

It was, however, the information which was received rather than that which was given *anent* the interests of education and religion in Calcutta and among the Bengalis generally, that was most worthy of mention and of permanent account. Almost every waking hour of the weeks spent in the city, when I was not myself engaged in speaking, was occupied under the escort and guidance of Mr. Kali Banurji, in getting an intimate acquaintance with the educational, social, and religious affairs of the natives of this capital of India. The impressions and inferences from impressions, instead of being strung in their exact order on the thread of time, will best be told by grouping them under several heads.

The first in the series of visits to the great number of educational institutions of various types which have been founded in Calcutta was to the Government College. Here we were met by the Principal and some of the professors and shown over the buildings. In this college the only person doing any work of research, or seeming to be interested in such work, was the young native professor of physics (he has since lectured on his discoveries in England and in this country) who was investigating the changes in the atomic structure of plant life caused by the agitation given them by the ether-waves. From here we drove to the City College, an institution founded in the interests of the Brahmo-Somaj. This four-storied building was extremely disorderly and dirty, and the attire of its indwellers, including the Principal, inclined strongly toward the disreputable. But it swarmed with alert and eager students to the number of 1,200 in all. The Sanskrit College next enlisted deserved attention. This institution was founded for high-caste Hindus exclusively. In its appointments, teachers and pupils, it was much more respectable in appearance than was the City College; but it is doubtful whether so much work of actual instruction and practical influence is being done there. Its collection of Sanskrit manuscripts is particularly large and valuable. As an unexampled honor and privilege, I was allowed to take into my unpurified hands two of the oldest ones,—written on palm-leaves, worm-eaten and fallen into decay, so that the merest touch of them was rather precarious. One of the two manuscripts was said to be 700 years old; the other had belonged to the king of Ceylon and dated back 800 years.

During another morning, three other colleges were exhibited and explained to us. Of these the first was the college for women on Cornwallis Square. This institution was then under the principalship of a Hindu lady, Miss Gose, a convert to Christianity and an M.A. of Calcutta University. The girls in the college classes are from either Christian or Brahmo-Somaj families, and many of them were pretty and intelligent young women. In contrast with this, the pupils of the Hindu College for girls, where little or no English is taught, were not only considerably younger,—since before they can get much education they are taken out of school to be married,—but also seemed decidedly inferior in physiognomy and bearing. The Government supplements the fees of this college, having "taken over" the institution, and the position of the Lady-Principal is well paid, since she has house and servants furnished, and a salary of three hundred rupees per month, with prospect of an increase up to seven hundred. Some thirty or forty girls are boarders and are lodged in two large dormitory rooms. They have native food; but, like Christians, eat on tables and sleep on beds.

From these schools for girls we were driven to the Free Church College, where Dr. Hector met us and conducted us over the buildings, answering freely all our more pressing inquiries. It is impossible to enforce with the Bengalis of the student class, in general and as long as they remain Hindus, any such discipline as distinguishes even our "looser" examples of the American college. As we passed through the rooms where the students lodged and were supposed to do their studying, many of them were lying on their beds, either with a neglected book before them or even fast asleep.

The next round of visitation took in the three principal native private colleges. The first of these, Central College, was founded by a graduate of the Free Church College, Mr. K. R. Bose, who greeted both his visitors with great cordiality and show of respect,—he having learned his philosophy of Mr.

Banurji. The entire support of this college comes from the fees of the pupils; but since the college is small, and the connected school of lower grades is relatively large,—as is the case of many of our Western institutions—the former draws its support in part from the surplus funds of the latter. From here we went to "Ripon College," which is so named because the school of lower grade developed into the college under the administration of Lord Ripon. This was, on the whole, the most remarkable educational institution I had ever visited. It is domiciled in a large, and what was formerly a very elegant house, built around a court; and in other low buildings occupying part of the compound back of the house. The corridors swarmed with students who had to be literally pushed out of the way in order that we might reach the den used as an office of administration, where the Principal was seated. He is said to be very popular and his pupils much devoted to him. As we were conducted about and introduced to teachers and students in room after room, the crowd of the "unemployed" followed us, gazing with the same open-eyed curiosity, and displaying the same stupid slowness about getting out of the way, which both men and bullocks manifested on the streets of the city. The corridors and recitation rooms themselves were all incredibly dirty; and some of them were so dark, damp, and obviously unsanitary that they would not pass inspection as cells in the common jail of any well-ordered American city. Including its Law-school, this institution numbers more than 1,600 students.

In the third and last place, we stopped at the Metropolitan College, where accommodations were rather better, at least as they appeared on the surface, than at the other native private schools.

The fees paid by the students at these so-called colleges range from two to five rupees (67 cents to $1.67) per month, the larger sum being charged by the missionary colleges. Of libraries and laboratories there were at that time practically none worth mentioning in the educational institutions of Calcutta, with the exception of the chemical and physical laboratories of the Government College. As specimens of the character and ambitions of a large multitude of those who come to attend these institutions, this selection, from a number recorded in my diary and in my memory may suffice. The son of the most distinguished of the native judges was studying for the B.A. degree in one of the missionary colleges affiliated with the Calcutta University. He had chosen Latin instead of Sanskrit for his second language, as much the easier and more convenient (*sic*) of the two. His so-called *study* of any foreign language was confined to committing to memory from a "crib" the translation of the passages assigned for the daily task. He complained to his father that his teacher was trying to compel him really to learn English, whereas all he wanted was to pass the examinations. This, since language counts 60 per cent for a pass-examination, and 25 per cent of correct answers is enough for a pass, is no serious task for the average boy to accomplish by mere dead-lift of memory without any substantial knowledge of the subject. But the rewards of the "pass" are in themselves *substantial.* For as between Calcutta papas when negotiating marriages, there is a definite scale of values affixed to the University degrees: e. g., a B.A. pass is worth R. 750; a B.A. honor, R 1,000; an M.A. counts for R. 1,500; and a B.L. has a value of R. 2,000-2,500. Even a B.A. failure to pass has a certain commercial value. But here, as elsewhere, the matrimonial market fluctuates in accordance with the law of supply and demand.

What is the product, and what are the effects in society and in state and church, of such a system of education as applied to the Bengalis? There can be little doubt that in many respects it is highly unsatisfactory.

In a conversation with the Viceroy, then Lord Curzon, I raised this question, although in rather an indirect and covert fashion; but it led to the complaint which was also voiced by Lady Curzon, that one of the most perplexing problems of Government was how to deal with the rapidly accumulating surplus of native *babus.* The conversation must have left some impression, for I received next day from the Viceroy's secretary—"written at his Excellency's command"—a letter of introduction to Mr. Pedlar, then Director of Education. In this letter it was mentioned that I was particularly interested in a better technical education for the natives. On visiting Mr. Pedlar I found him needing no argument to enforce the conviction that the current system of university education in India was unfitting most of the candidates for degrees, for the life they must lead after leaving the university. They "will not work," said he; "they will not put their brains into their hands or their hands to any work more distinctly manual than handling a pen or the papers in some government office." Mr. Pedlar declared that the educated government clerk would not even carry up-stairs from the street cars in front of the government offices a chronometer or other small package for which he had been sent. The educated *babu* believes himself to have a right to demand employment in some "gentlemanly" pursuit; and all his poor relations believe that he is bound to share with them, so that they may work less or need not work at all, the fruits of these *labors* (?). (The day before, my wife had discovered our traveling native companion making the bed by the way of sitting in an arm-chair by the bedside and gently and leisurely patting the sheets.)

The attitude of the same class of minds toward religion in general, and toward Christianity in particular, is illustrated in the following letter—one of a considerable collection—which was written by a Calcutta *babu* to one of the missionaries situated some hundreds of miles from that city. I copy it as it was written.

"Venerable Father,

"A *Sudra* by birth I have suffered much from the Selfish principals of the Brahmins. This & a knowledge of the Sins of Idolatry have led my mind to the immediate resignation of Hinduism.

"Then what religion to accept? I prefer Christianity to all those that ever exist under the Sun.

"But to tell the truth Father, the Sorrowful tears of my parents, to whom I am the only prop and who are greatly entangled by the Satan of debt, put an obstacle to my being a convert. I, a student, instead of helping them in their difficulties, Shamelessly ask help from them for the continuation of my Studies. In this way getting more and more indebted, they are to lose what they have and on which the Support of our family Solely depends.

"Then Kind Father, if you receive me as your own son, and give me the best education you can afford for the improvement of my deplorable condition, I unscrupulously accept Christianity and devote my life to its *Holiness*. Hoping you will not do otherwise than return a favorable reply soon.

"I remain
Kind Father
your unfortunate Son,
Kailas Chander Sarkar."

Let it not be supposed, however, that this description applies to all the educated natives among the Bengalis or throughout all India. There, in Calcutta, were several score of highly educated men who had not "unscrupulously" accepted Christianity, but who, remaining Brahmans, were taking a part worthy of educated men in the civil and social work and improvement of the community. There were more who, like Mr. Kali Banurji, had been really "converted" in heart and life to the religion of Christ, and who were doing valiant and self-denying and effective service in its behalf; and still more, of the humbler sort who were living as best they knew how in the performance of unnoticed daily duties, "for his name's sake." And, then, there were the professed social and religious reformers—some wholly sincere and well enlightened, and some not so sincere and more ignorant or self-deluded—who were stirring up themselves and one another, and trying to stir up the community, in behalf of a large improvement of social morals and religious beliefs and practices. Through their extraordinary courtesy toward me, and their implicit confidence in my friendly escort, very special opportunities were afforded for an acquaintance with the Brahmo-Somaj and similar or rival organizations.

The visit to the home of the Brahmo-Somaj people, which occupied the forenoon of January 16, 1900, is worthy of a somewhat detailed account.

We called first upon Protab Chunder Mazumdar, the successor—so far as any one could be said to have been at that time recognized as such—of Keshub Chunder Sen, and found him apparently expecting us, seated at his table in the room which he uses as a study. Mazumdar is a rather striking man, with iron-grey hair and pleasing features. There is, however, a marked sensuousness about his countenance; and his critics accuses him, not without grounds, of too much high-flown rhetoric and ambiguity of language, with at least occasional acts of duplicity. He showed in our brief conversation a quite too exalted estimate of the contributions of Hinduism to the purest and highest form of religion, and of the superiority in religious and philosophical thought of the Oriental mind. Mozumdar seemed very earnest in his invitation to attend his annual sermon which was to be preached in the Town Hall next Saturday afternoon on the subject, "The Contributions of the Orient to the West." He evidently wished me to appear upon the platform.

We then walked the few steps necessary to bring us to "Lily Cottage," the home of the great reformer Keshub Chunder Sen, where we met his son, grandson, and a number of the missionaries of the Brahmo-Somaj. Mr. Sen took us first to see the marble monuments in an enclosure which is protected from the birds by a wire cage, and where are the ashes of his father and his mother. Keshub Chunder Sen's monument has the same inscription on all four sides, but repeated in Sanskrit, Persian, Bengali and English. It is his own celebrated sentence about the flight of the little "bird I,"—the soul.

Near by, but in a separate enclosure, are the monuments of young Mr. Sen's wife and infant son. After this, we visited the chapel where, facing the outside door of the entrance, is the somewhat raised platform on which as his pulpit Keshub Chunder Sen used to sit and preach. Since his death this seat of the teacher's authority has never been occupied; and the question whether it shall be left vacant or not, *in perpetuo*, has been the occasion of a split in the Brahmo-Somaj. Just "at his feet," in front and at the sides, sat the apostles or more devoted pupils and missionaries of his doctrine. Each of them had his special mat which he brought and took away with him. Two of the missionaries showed me theirs, —one a goatskin, the other a woolen rug which, he said, was the gift of "the master" himself. At the present time, since it was a festival occasion, all the space immediately surrounding the platform was decorated with flowers,—not at all, however, as we should decorate, but by laying the blossoms upon the floor in symbolical, geometrical and other patterns. The remoter parts of the room, which was in all perhaps 24 ft. square, were for the occupancy of the less distinguished members of the church.

The instruments on which the musical part of the

Brahmo-Somaj's religious service was performed were—at least so far as they were shown to me—a large drum shaped like an hour-glass, and several pairs of cymbals. In their processions, their music was animated and stirring (as I had occasion to know by the disturbance of my lectures),—"So and So," as my informant illustrated by beating the drum with his hands. But in their meetings by themselves, where the elect came together for meditation and prayer, the music is low and soft. The bible of the Brahmo-Somaj was then shown to me. It contains selections from various religious books, including, of course, the Old and New Testaments. The principle of selection seems to have been whatever struck the fancy of the person who made the selection. Keshub Chunder Sen used to discourse at considerable length in these meetings, although the meetings themselves were appointed especially for meditation and prayer.

We were taken from the Chapel back into the house; and first into the drawing-room, on the walls of which hung two portraits in oil of the departed master, and a photograph of Queen Victoria presented to him with an autograph copy of her Majesty's book, "Leaves from My Journal."

Almost immediately the screen in front of the adjoining bedroom was folded aside by young Mr. Sen, who had slipped off his shoes reverently before approaching any spot sacred to the memory of his

Father, and we were beckoned to see where "*he* breathed his last." The bedroom was small, but furnished with two single beds set close side by side, in the one of which nearest the door Keshub Chunder Sen had died. A white sheet was spread over the bed and over a long bolster lying lengthwise in the middle, which gave the appearance of a dead body just about to be prepared for burial. The son explained that his father's room had been left just as it was when he died, "except so far as necessary for tidiness." A little piece of carpentry which he had made in his last illness was shown; and also the family heirloom in the shape of a brass flagon with a long spout, out of which the sick man had drunk when he was too ill to raise himself in bed.

On returning to the drawing-room I was introduced to Keshub Chunder Sen's mother, an aged lady of more than eighty, who through her grandson thanked me for the honor done her in calling, although she knew it was rather due to the excellence of her departed son. With the most perfect simplicity, sincerity and earnestness, the dear old lady assured me that now, and for many years in the past, her only consolation had been the religious faith to which her son had devoted his life. When I bade her good-bye, she graciously bestowed upon me her maternal blessing.

As we went through the front yard to reach our garry, we were shown the tank which gave the name of "Lily Cottage" to the house; in which Keshub Chunder Sen was himself baptized by one of the brethren; and in which all the members admitted to this branch of the Brahmo-Somaj are now baptized,—in "name of the Father, the Son, and the Holy Ghost." Mr. Banurji said that, although the reformer was in the beginning of his career oftentimes bitter toward Christianity, he came finally not only to have a sincere reverence for Christ, but also to regard him as in a special and unique sense the revealer of the true religion and *the* son of God. The general moral and religious atmosphere of this branch of the Somaj, he thought to be very excellent. They employ in all some sixteen or eighteen missionaries, but there is little growth to their avowed membership. The latest available statistics gave the total numbers of the Somaj adherents in all India at somewhat more than six thousand. But, as one of the missionaries of the order asserted, they did not rely on or greatly value statistics, but wished to elevate the people by diffusing true ideas and a devout spirit.

There was much in all I saw and learned of the Brahmo-Somaj which, in other centuries, would undoubtedly have served as the beginning for the worship of another deified man,—the initiation of a new god. But Mr. Banurji, who admitted that there had been at one time danger of deifying Keshub Chunder Sen, thought this danger to be now successfully passed. It must be remembered, however, that in the case of all the branches of the Somaj movement, as among the Orientals generally, the attitude of heart and life toward the founders and leaders of religious sects, and toward the revered dead of the family, much more nearly resembles the worship fitly bestowed on the Divine Being than is the case with us Westerners.

From Lily Cottage we were driven to the house of Mr. Bose, who was then the intellectual and social leader of the other branch of the Brahmo-Somaj. Mr. Bose, who was educated in England, is a very cultivated gentleman and successful barrister, and the favorite with the student classes. One sees in him at once the keenly intellectual and polished man of the world; on the other hand the devout and reverent atmosphere of Lily Cottage is here wanting, or at least not so obvious.

On the way home we stopped at the missionary house of the Brahmo-Somaj. It was a dark and dirty and rather dilapidated structure in an obscure lane. But the brethren were very cordial, and I sat and talked with them so long, and waited so in acquiescence to their demand that I should not depart until I had "sweetened my mouth" in their house, that I was very late to luncheon.

More private interviews with individual visitors of the various branches of the reformed sects served to deepen and correct the impressions with which I had begun my travels in India. One morning a missionary of the more orthodox branch of the Brahmo-Somaj, who had more of a reputation among his brethren for his piety than for his learning or intellectual vigor, called to inquire about the possibility of his coming to the United States to study religion further. This brother seemed to have no objection to the views or the theological dogma of the "Philosophical" Christian Trinitarians.

Another morning, just as we were sitting down to breakfast, two natives called and announced themselves as emissaries of the Chaitanya Somaj. They talked so rapidly and in such broken and poor English, and interrupted each other so frequently, that I had great difficulty in gathering what they really wished. By point-blank questioning, however, it was discovered that they wanted to arrange a meeting for me with the leader of the sect and editor of its paper, "Patrika." They left in my hands a circular advertising two volumes by Shishir Kumar Ghose, on "Lord Gauranga, or Salvation for All." In this circular, Ghose's book, together with other worthless stuff from Madame Blavatsky and others of her ilk, was especially commended by "Professor Buchanan of America, the Discoverer of Psychometry." I had previously supposed that Fechner and Weber had something to do with this discovery. But the secrets of "soul-measurement" as known to those initiated in the Indian theosophy are not for plain and ordinary Western minds.

In this connection it is pertinent to mention the

opinion of Mr. Kali Banurji—than whom, as has already been indicated, no one could be more competent to judge—that on the whole the influence of the so-called "Parliament of Religions" held in this country had been bad in India. In one case, the leader of a vile sect which continues phallic worship and the lewdest practices connected with it, had returned to strut about and brag of his seat in the Parliament as on a par with those of representatives of the Brahmo-Somaj and of Christianity.

Before setting out on our trip around the world we had received a very cordial introduction to Lady Curzon from her father, Mr. Leiter, of Chicago. This kindness procured us several invitations to Government House, the most prized of which was an invitation to luncheon where we were the only guests besides the members of the family. When Lord and Lady Curzon appeared in the waiting-room, where we had been conversing with one of his aide-de-camps, the Viceroy immediately said: "Let us go out to luncheon," and himself led the way. Before reaching the table, however, he fell back to speak with Mrs. Ladd, who was then seated on his right; while Lady Curzon proceeded to her chair and invited me to a seat on her right. Her conversation with me, after a few general questions asked and answered, concerned the ever-increasing swarm of *babus* who get, or just fail in getting, a university degree; and who then find no mission in life beyond trying for some government office. This conversation, which was continued with the Viceroy, in a small room partitioned off from the verandah, over the after-dinner coffee, led to the result of which sufficient has already been said.

Lord Curzon made upon me an excellent impression as having a fine blend of accurate information, good sense, and principled kindness. It was also interesting to find that he had a pretty thorough acquaintance with, and a very good opinion of, the Japanese. The impression made by the American woman he had married had already won for her the admiration and affection of all classes in India.

Some time later we were invited to a dinner at Government House, at which seventy guests were at table, and which was followed by a dance to which three times that number were invited. The lady who was assigned to my escort I discovered—but only the next day—to be Mrs. Cotes, the author of "A Social Adventure," "The Simple Adventures of a Mem Sahib," and other books, under the *nom de plume* of Sarah Jeanette Duncan. But since all her conversation was with a young officer, who sat on her right, about the Boer war, this ignorance did not matter. On this occasion also the Viceroy and Lady Curzon appeared in the reception-room only after all the guests were assembled. But at length one of the aide-de-camps announced "Their Excellencies," when they at once entered and passed in front of the entire assembly "lined up," as the saying is, extending a hand to each without speaking,—Lady Curzon some three or four steps behind her husband. The gentlemen all bowed; the ladies courtsied. They then led the way to the dinner table, the Viceroy taking out the wife of the Governor of Bengal, and Lady Curzon escorted by Chief Justice Maclean. These details of etiquette are referred to, not for their intrinsic importance in the sight of the "plain American Citizen," but because they are really of no small importance in the effect they have upon the attitude of the Oriental toward the individual or the nation that observes or neglects them.

Two or three dinner-table incidents will throw some light on the customs and sentiments that have much to do with the control of British India. A member of the French Embassy had a violent nose bleed which he strove in vain to staunch before being compelled to leave the table. When he was finally forced to withdraw, he left his bloodstained napkin lying in the chair. Not one of the Mussulman waiters in their long red robes would touch it, and the slightly disagreeable task was forced upon one of the English head-butlers.

Toward the close of the dinner, as the Viceroy stood and said: "To the Queen Empress," all rose to their feet and drank to Her Majesty's health by at least touching the glass to the lips. One very abstemious English lady on the opposite side of the table, who had refused to take wine with any of the courses, became the object of no little amusement to those who understood the language of the waiter, as he overcame her resistance to having the glass of port poured out for her, only by saying repeatedly in Hindustani and in tones of increasing anxiety: "The Queen will be drunk; the Queen will be drunk."

At the ball which followed in the state apartment over the dining room, after dancing the *quadrille d'honneur* "Their Excellencies" took no further part; but withdrew to the room just over the throne-room, where they remained and had summoned to them such persons only as they wished to meet. At 11:30 they retired and thus left free such of their guests as desired to come away.

Less "distinguished" but more enjoyable than the "function" just described were the receptions given to us at the houses of our hosts, Doctor and Mrs. Hector and Professor and Mrs. Tomory. At the latter gathering which came near the end of our stay in Calcutta, there were present representatives of all the classes who had been more or less actively interested in the lectures and various other addresses which I had given in the city; and thus there was a very desirable opportunity to attempt something like a fair estimate of the results obtained. It was especially comforting to note that Mr. Banurji and a Mr. Maden, who spoke of himself as "a poor cot-ten-spinner," although he had been introduced as the "Calcutta Mr. Tata," or merchant prince, seemed in agreement on this point.

During the stay in Calcutta several extraordinary opportunities occurred to see in a more intimate way some of the more ridiculous and some of the more cruel and loathsome sides of orthodox Hinduism. In the former class may best be put the visit which Mrs. Ladd was permitted to make with us to a family of *Pirati* or "polluted" Brahmans. The tradition is that more than one hundred years ago one of the ancestors of this family—whether on compulsion or voluntarily, the tradition is divided—ate of, or at least smelled of, Muhammadan roast beef. Refusing to get absolution by doing the required costly penance, the entire family became and have since remained outcasted. It costs them a pretty penny to get sons-in-law and daughters-in-law; for any girl marrying into the family can never return to her home. She, too, becomes an outcast. But the family have become rich, since their large compound has now been made central by the growth of the city of Calcutta, and is surrounded by very profitable bazaars. They have also multiplied largely and have arrived at a size to form a sort of a caste of their own, and to hire Brahmans to join them and perform all the rites of Hinduism. The sons of the last Maharajah—for they seem to have a right to claim this title—became a Christian, and his father disinherited him. The present head of the family is an old gentleman who was a nephew and who became the heir to the estate and the title by a will which was disputed but upheld by the native court in India. The case was appealed to a judicial committee of the Privy Council, who decided that upon the present incumbent's death the estate must revert to the lineal descendants.

The house in which the outcast, Sir Maharajah Jotindra Mhun Tagore, lives is one of the most magnificent of the native houses in Calcutta. As usual with such houses, however, its surroundings were filthy and squalid. We were met near the entrance by two handsome and well-dressed young Hindus and shown up into a drawing-room which, for size and magnificence of some of its furnishings, was truly royal. But there was here the same mixture of meanness and magnificence which had characterized the surroundings. The Maharajah was at his breakfast; and while we were waiting for him, the young men entertained us by setting a-going a large Swiss music-box. When the old gentleman appeared, arrayed in an elegant Cashmire shawl for his morning dress, we found him very cordial, bright, and entertaining.

Did the most intelligent of the orthodox Hindus really approve of such ridiculous ways of distinguishing truth from error and dividing up the family of God into innumerable castes and outcasts?

This was the question raised by our visit to the Maharajah Tagore. Our next call provided the question with a practical answer. For it was upon one of the most highly educated, liberal and kindly of the strictly orthodox Hindus. While my wife and her female attendant were visiting the zenana, the doctor talked with me of his practice, of the affliction he had recently met in the loss of his wife and a favorite son, and of his hope of a reunion with his loved ones in heaven, with all the sincerity of faith and devoutness of feeling which could possibly characterize a "good Christian." Yet when he learned from whose house we had come to his, he declared that nothing could induce him to allow a member of his family to cross a threshold so accursed. In what essential respects, however, do these attitudes of Hinduism differ from those prevalent in so-called Christian circles during the centuries of their history?

Of the cynical side of some Hindus a very vivid impression was gained when we responded to the formal invitation to visit in his office the editor of the *Patrika* and the author of the two-volumed work on "Lord Gauranga or Salvation for All." Mounting with some difficulty a dirty, dark and winding staircase, we found in his diminutive den an emaciated man with a mixture of conceit, fanaticism, and craft in his bearing; and yet with a certain pathetic earnestness. Mr. Ghose began at once to complain of the powerlessness of all religion, especially Christianity, to accomplish anything in the way of a practical and ethical communion of man with God. The philosophical views which he alone understood thoroughly and had expounded in his two-volumed treatise would be found the only means effective in producing this highly desirable result.

But it was a visit to the Kali Ghat which gave just a glimpse into some of the most cruel and repulsive and obscene ceremonies and practices possible in the Hindu cult. Of the worship of this "ferocious she-monster" a modern writer (Professor Hopkins) has said: "Obscenity is the soul of this cult. Bestiality equalled only by the orgies of the Indic savages among the hill-tribes is the form of this religion. . . . A description of the different rites would be to reduplicate an account of indecencies, of which the least vile is too esoteric to sketch faithfully."

This temple of the goddess Kali is seated on the old bank of the Ganges a few miles from the city of Calcutta; the place derives its sanctity from the legend that when the corpse of Shiva's wife was cut in pieces by order of the gods, one of her fingers fell on this spot. The approaches to this temple are lined with bazaars, many of which are filled with wares of different sorts connected with the worship of Kali. On alighting from the garry we were at once surrounded by a crowd of dirty beggars crying out for *backshish.* We gave ourselves into the hands of a young priest who was comparatively neatly dressed, but who had in an exaggerated degree all the irritating characteristics of the oily, conceited, and superficial Bengali. He proved a good conductor, however,—but only so far as our physical leadership was concerned; for he showed that he really knew nothing when we came to ask as to the origin and essential nature of Kali worship.

Just as we reached the place where the sacrifices were performed, a goat was being fastened into the arrangement for holding its head firm; and in a trice with a single blow (it is bad luck not to have a single blow do this work neatly) it was beheaded and its headless body carried off kicking vigorously. The sights and smells were so disconcerting to the ladies of the party that they wished to draw back without giving further opportunity for investigation in the interests of comparative religion; but they were persuaded to keep on until we could be shown around the entire outside of the temple structures. Into the temple itself none but qualified Hindus may enter. We were shown the bathing-tank which is connected with the Ganges by a canal, in the filth-laden waters of which perhaps a score of people were engaged in bathing. The young priest assured us that these waters were sacred and used only for sacred purposes. We could well believe it, for in India no other waters are so disgustingly and dangerously filthy as

THE FILTH-LADEN WATERS

those used for purposes of religious purification. According to his story, worshippers came to this temple of Kali from all over India, bringing offerings to be sacrificed, of goats and sheep and buffalo.

As we came away the beggars "pitched into" us again. One especially persistent fellow wished us to give to him, above all others, because he was a priest and a gentleman; and an able-bodied, well-nourished boy ran beside our vehicle for nearly a mile, crying out, "Sahib, Sahib, backshish, backshish."

The narrative of our experiences in Calcutta may fitly be brought to a close by a word or two regarding some of the more interesting and instructive of the excursions made from the city. Of these, one consisted of a sail down the river to the Botanical Gardens, where, that day, no fewer than four church-picnics were being held. We visited the celebrated huge Banyan tree, which was then 129 years old, and had a circumference of 51 ft. of trunk at 5½ ft. from the ground; and of its crown, a circumference of 930 ft. This tree had already 417 serial roots actually established in the ground beneath. The process of inducing new roots to grow just where their support is most needed is interesting. The tree is scarified and the new root is taken down to the ground inside of a bamboo support which has been filled with soil.

The Jain temple of Calcutta, with its surrounding gardens and their variegated pavements, with its tinsel and glass and inlaid work, was worth a brief visit. But we were fortunate in having previously visited the temple of the same sect in Ahmedabad under intelligent guidance; for the fellow who showed us around and called himself by the absurd title, "a Jain-Hindu" (Jain, in order to hold his place and get his Rupee; and Hindu, in order to keep his caste and save himself from social inconvenience) was totally unqualified for his business. He did not even know what the word Tirthankar meant. The priests were Hindus, serving for what they could make out of it; and the only person about the premises who appeared to know anything whatever about Jainism was a young man not connected with the temple, who, with his older companion, turned out to be pilgrims from Bombay.

On one of the Saturdays, with a congenial company, we had a delightful sail up the river as far as opposite Barakpore. Just as we were setting out on the return journey, the government launch carrying the servants, followed by one carrying the Viceroy, Lady Curzon, and a party of friends, met us on the way to his summer-house for an over-Sunday.

After having such pleasant times and making so many good friends in Calcutta, it is not strange that when late in January we parted from them on the platform of the station and knew we should have small chance of seeing them again, we felt a distinct tug on the heart-strings. Although our car was uncommonly good in its appointments, there was little sleep for me that night, partly from the excitement of bidding farewell and partly from anxiety over news threatening the work in the homeland.

CHAPTER VIII

HOLY BENARES

THE City of Benares, or *Kasi* (the "Bright" [?]) as the Hindus commonly call it, has been the religious capital of India from far back of historic times. Indeed, authentic history of the past of this ancient and important center of Indian religious life is very deficient, although it is certain that it was flourishing six centuries before the Christian era; for it was then that Sakya Muni, the founder of Buddhism, came to establish his religion there. And Buddha died at the age of eighty about 480 B. C. Even the site of the ancient city is in some doubt, for it was several times changed; and the present city is constantly slipping away into the treacherous but sacred river that runs at the foot of the high bank on which are situated many of the most gorgeous of its ancient temples and palaces. Under Moslem rule its religious institutions suffered terribly. It is recorded that one of the Mogul generals destroyed a thousand temples and built mosques in their places. But no political pressure or military violence has availed to destroy the religious pre-eminence in the Hindu mind, of Holy Benares. We were then obliged to visit it on this account; and also because we had talking of an unusually interesting character—at least, to ourselves—to do in the religious capital of India.

At the Benares Cantonment station we were met by our host and given a most cordial welcome. Immediately after luncheon we got ready for a so-called *conversazione* in the garden, at which some twenty gentlemen, mostly professors in the Hindu and Queens Colleges, were present. The conversation was general; but one of the Hindus took me aside to ask what I thought Christ meant when he said, "I and my Father are one." After I had explained my understanding of the words he remarked that the Vedanta philosophy had much earlier taught the same truth. When questioned, however, as to his conception of the nature of this human oneness with the Divine Being he showed what all Oriental speculation on such problems of theology and philosophy always shows,—a very marked difference from the western thought as to what can properly be meant by personality and by personal relations.

A more marked and almost startling example of the difference to which reference was just made, was afforded the next morning by a lengthy conversation with the "ascetic Raja Bhinga, the man of whom Dr. Fairbairn published such a superlative estimate in the *Contemporary Review* on his return from his lecturing tour in India. Raja Bhinga lives in a bungalow fully two miles distant from the London Mission. And since our call was set for seven o'clock in the morning, early rising and a hurried *chota hazri* were the conditions of keeping the engagement. A servant on guard with an old-fashioned musket was stationed at the gateway. Sending in our cards we were immediately asked to enter and meet the owner in his small drawing-room.

Raja Bhinga appeared to be about fifty years of age. He had a distinctly intellectual face which in conversation lighted up with a pleasant smile,—touched with occasional gleams of sarcasm and tender bitterness. The Raja is an ascetic and a believer in the higher Hinduism; but his asceticism does not assume a repulsive physical form. His dress was plain but free from any peculiarities designed to attract to itself the attention either of the wearer or of others.

The views of either Protestant or Romanist orthodoxy could not differ more from those of Kuenen and Wellhausen regarding the Old Testament and the clergy than did those of Raja Bhinga regarding the Vedas and the Hindu priesthood from those which I had heard expressed several months before by the Shankarā-chāryā of the Kapola Bania caste in Bombay. In respect of all the Vedic writings and the commentaries upon them,—Upanishads, Puranas, etc.,—the Raja declared himself a thorough skeptic and rationalist. Even the most ancient of the Vedas were, in his judgment, full of "admixtures" and contained only occasional truths together with much that was "rubbish" and erroneous. True and higher Hinduism rejects not only the infallibility of the Scriptures but also the claims of the Brahmans. These priests, though pretending to teach the people with authority and even claiming from them reverence and worship, are blind leaders of the blind. The interpretations of the pundits have no great value. The revival of the Yoga philosophy now current is not true Yoga philosophy, is gaining few adherents, and is of little or no valuable influence. The Theosophists are more numerous hereabouts; but most of them do not know what they mean and can only captivate silly women and boys (this was a decided rap at Madame Blavatsky and Mrs. Besant). The Hindu Central College of Benares has started out to give a religious education to the sons of the higher caste Hindus; but the Brahmans will have their own way there, and the pundits will teach their own biased views; and no real enlightenment will result.

When questioned as to his own religious views Raja Bhinga spoke frankly and in delightfully clear and elegant English. He avowed his belief in the doctrine of Māyā or "The Great Illusion": even the teachings and scheme of the Vedas, and all the Brahmanical philosophy and liturgy, as well as the world of things, belongs to the sphere of illusion. All is Māyā.

The world is full of evil, so the ascetic Raja of

Holy Benares went on to explain. Pain is the fundamental, the universal, the ineradicable experience. It cannot be banished or overcome so long as one remnant of Māyā remains. But there are two ways in which a true Hindu may conduct himself toward this pain of existence. He may withdraw as much as possible from the world and give himself up to reflection; or he may for duty's sake endure the world while taking no pleasure in it,—may go about this city, while being a true citizen of another and heavenly city. The way of self-denial is the only Way of Salvation. It is the extinction of all desire, of all love of self, of all interest in self, which at last brings the true believer to Nirvāna.

But what is Nirvāna? How shall we describe this supreme good which the righteous man attains, who follows the Path of Salvation? Is it the extinction of all consciousness? No, for then a man might attain it by getting very drunk or falling into a fainting fit. Is it then the extinction of self-consciousness? Certainly, yes; for the extinction of the very root of self-interest is the only way of salvation. Questioned as to how a "person" could be said to be saved, that was no longer a *person*, having lost the indispensable characteristic of personality, the Raja claimed that the English language did not afford the words necessary to make clear his conception of Nirvāna. And since I could not argue with him about subtle distinctions in philosophical Sanskrit, we seemed to be at an *empasse* in our efforts to agree with each other.

On our way homeward we stopped at the "monkey temple," in the garden of which a quite different kind of ascetic had practiced for many years, receiving visitors and gathering their autographs. The old swami, who acquired the title of *the* "holy man" of Benares, was said to have been a simple-hearted, sincere, devout, but ignorant person; but his successor looked as though he had gone into the business of saintship for what it might be worth. The marble effigy of the departed saint, near by the cagelike enclosure in which he is said to have been buried, represents him in the attitude in which he used to pose during his lifetime; and here he is already worshipped as divine, so little time does it take to make a new god in India.

It may be doubted whether a more desperate and concentrated plunge downward from the heights of religious contemplation and attempt at pure living to the most loathsome and obscene superstitions that deceive the minds and deprave the morals of mankind under the name of religion, could anywhere be found than that which one takes who passes, not as an unthinking listener or sightseer, but as an intelligent and thoughtful observer, from the presence of Raja Bhinga to the so-called "Monkey Temple" of Benares. For what the Europeans call by this impromptu title, because of the myriads of monkeys which infest the large trees nearby, is more properly called the "Durga Temple," as consecrated to the goddess of that name. But Durga is the terrific form of Shiva's wife; and Durga is the concentrated essence, so to say, of everything silly, obscene, and cruel, which a foul imagination can picture as belonging to the *Female* (*das Weibliche*), when endowed with power, unrestrained either by fear of superior physical force or by semblance of moral considerations. Durga is the Female Devil, raging with cruelty and lust, let loose. Her worship is a Bacchic orgy, with unlimited indulgence in "wine and women." Human sacrifices were formerly among its bloody rites. Today, under fear of Government, the lust for blood is "appeased by the hacking of their own bodies," and by cutting off the heads of goats. Their sanguinary tribute to the terrible wife of Shiva may be seen sprinkled about this Durga Temple, in whose groves monkeys ceaselessly chatter and gambol. Other lusts are not appeased in so limited a way.

The following day was occupied in going about the holy city. We drove first to a point well up the Ganges and there hired one of those queer boats which ply up and down the river. Chairs were placed on the tarred roof of the dark little cabin; and the four oarsmen started to row us down the stream in front of the bathing- and burning-ghats, and the medley of temples and palaces which line the upper part of the eastern bank of the Ganges. Numbers of citizens and pilgrims were in the different stages of the act of acquiring merit or doing penance by bathing in its sacred waters. The ascetics who were not thus engaged were squatting in the openings of their cells or in the open air. Among the bathers were fat old men and fat old women, children of both sexes, youths and maidens. The males seemed quite indifferent to the various degrees of exposure which their morning exercise involved; but some of the maidens and younger women showed conscious glances from dark and handsome eyes, and made haste to gather their *saris* about their bodies or their breasts. And, indeed, "the eternal feminine" is essentially the same the world over. For had we not noticed on the streets of Bombay that when the driver of the garry wished a woman who persisted in walking in front of his horse, to get out of the way, he cried out, "*ghullau margary. Mhan-ta-ree*" ("Get back, old woman"), at which the veiled one, if she was really young, pulled the veil aside to demonstrate how inapplicable was the implied insult. Most of the bathers were shivering with the cold; for although pith hats are needed in this part of India to protect one against the winter's sun, the nights and early mornings are cool enough to make bathing in the open air a veritable penance for the native's sensitive skin. A few were ostensibly praying; fewer still showed signs of really being absorbed in their devotions.

The shrines and temples along the bank had an

abundance of "offerings" in and around them,—mostly of flowers; but of them all not another displayed so many gifts of floral sort, or so many pies (a copper coin of the value of about one-quarter of a cent) lying on the floor or being counted by the priests, as did the shrine devoted to the worship of the goddess of smallpox. A veritable species of devil-worship this.

The upper burning-ghat had as yet no funeral pyre lighted and no corpse brought down to it after being made ready for cremation. But by the time we had reached the lower and more popular burning-ghat, the business of the day was well begun. One pyre had already been lighted and beside it stood a man feeding it with bundles of straw; for the wood seemed green and much in need of coaxing. In the water of the sacred river, near by the spot where the fire was smouldering, a dead body was floating, while it waited to be raised from its watery grave and committed to the arms of the friendly pyre, when that should have been sufficiently strengthened for its office. The boat was halted a moment and brought nearer to the bank that we might the better witness these obsequies. And now two men bearing a rudely constructed bamboo litter with a corpse swathed in white cotton, came trotting down into the water and slid off their burden dexterously from its lowered frame. Then one of them tore away the cotton coverings from the face and poured and dashed with

ON THE BANK ABOVE THE BURNING GHAT

his hands some of the purifying Ganges' waters upon the exposed head of the corpse. When we were returning by the place on foot—for we got out of the boat just above the Railway bridge and took it again much farther up the river,—we saw one body being consumed on the now fiercely burning funeral pyre, and several others waiting for their turn. In passing the *ghat*, one of the attendants was seen to seize upon one of the corpses "lying around," so to say, and was heard to cry out in the most matter-of-fact way: "Whose body is this?"

On the bank above the burning ghat, in the form of successive terraces of human beings, were crowds, some of whom were bargaining, some chattering gossip, some looking unconcernedly on.

The impressions made by the buildings of Benares as they lie along the upper bank, and as seen from the river, are not nearly so much of magnificence and solemnity as the photographs indicate. A few of these buildings, especially of the private houses of the Rajas, are really imposing; or, the rather, they *have been* imposing, for most of them have fallen into a pitiable state of decay. The most truly impressive feature still remaining is often the high flight of broad stone steps which leads down from the foundation walls to the edge of the river. The clay bank on this side of the Ganges is being constantly and rapidly eaten away; and indeed, it would seem to be only a question of time when all this part of Benares will be in ruins. In many parts of the bank the lower portions of the steps and of the foundation walls are already undermined and fallen. One building of much more than average magnificence, before it was finished, began to slide down the bank toward and into the river.

Our boat-ride finished, we wandered through some of the thickest parts of the city situated on the banks just over the Ganges. Anapurna, or "The Temple of Plenty," "The Golden Temple" dedicated to *Bisheshwar*, the "poison god," or Shiva, the famous Gyan Kup or "Well of Knowledge," which is situated in the quadrangle between the mosque and the Temple of Bisheshwar, as though to court the favor of Hindus and Moslems alike (for, surely, both and all men need to drink of the well of knowledge), and a half-score of other unassorted temples and ghats, were given a passing visit. Of all these, perhaps, Gyan Kup is most horribly and disgustingly fascinating. As to its attractions let us quote the unemotional but not untruthful or impious description of Murray's Hand-Book. "The quadrangle itself is unpleasant, but in that respect falls short of the well, which is absolutely fetid, from the decaying flowers thrown into it, notwithstanding that it has a grating over it, overspread with a cloth; for in this cloth there are large gaps, and flowers are continually falling through them. The votaries also throw down water; and as they are not at all particular how they throw it, they make the pavement one vast puddle, and besprinkle their fellow worshippers all over, so that the clothes of many of them are in a dripping state. . . . The platform is thronged by men and women, and the horrible din of gongs and voices deafens the visitor. Crowds of fresh pilgrims arrive incessantly; and as numbers of cows are mixed up in the throng, and must be treated with great consideration, the jostling is something terrific." The guide-book very properly omits mentioning the contributions made to the attractions of this "Well of Knowledge" by the human and bovine animals who crowd its sacred precincts.

But Gyan Kup is only all this part of India's chief holy city, concentrated within a few square yards. The streets of this section of Holy Benares, paved with flagging and not more than five or six feet wide, are winding lanes, dank and slippery and disgustingly filthy beyond the worst Western examples. They are crowded, not only with human beings, themselves filthy and half-naked, but with goats and cows and bullocks, which have equal rights of way with men and women; noisy with the chaffer of trade and the gossip and wrangling of worshippers. More physically repulsive than the pest houses and the famine camps are the ghats and temples of the city which is the center of the popular worship of native India. If there were any moral seriousness, of which there is so much in the Buddhist temples of Japan, to be discovered beneath these physically disgusting aspects of the "holiness" to be sought and found in this religious capital of the millions of Hinduism, one might pardon much, if not all, of that which is so offensive to nose and ears and eyes. But the amount of such seriousness, if any of it exist, is not obviously large.

In the evening of the same day, however, I had an experience of the "higher Hinduism," although of the type of which the Raja Bhinga had spoken with such marked contempt, that helped in a measure to redeem the impressions of the morning hours. The lecture was given under the auspices of the Central Hindu College, which was opened in 1898, and therefore only about a year before our visit. This institution was founded to give the higher-caste Hindus an education in Sanskrit and in the mysteries of their religion. Its beginnings were in the hands of the Theosophists, with Mrs. Besant as its patroness and a Dr. Richardson as its Principal. They were just then building a recitation-hall with sixteen rooms, and near by a home for Mrs. Besant, and another for the Principal. But the building in which the lecture was to be given was of a quite different origin, intention, and architecture. It had been intended by the previous Raja to be used as a summer palace. But before the palace was completed, it was struck by lightning; and this the superstitious owner interpreted as a sign from the gods that the completion of the palace would be unacceptable to them. His son had given it over to the Central Hindu College, with considerable adjoining land, in perpetuity. Its Hall of Audience had been nearly completed when the fateful stroke from heaven came, vetoing its further adornment. The hall was two lofty stories high, and around three sides of it ran galleries supported by arches on beautiful slender pillars of a mixed Saracenic and Hindu architecture. A platform had been placed in the middle of the long high decorated wall at the rear of this audience chamber, and on this the lecturer was to stand while speaking.

The extraordinary weirdness of that address, to such an audience and in such surroundings, will not easily pass from memory. There were no means of lighting the hall, except by the candles and lanterns which some of the audience had brought with them to guide their own footsteps or the drivers of their conveyances. These did not even serve to make the darkness visible, as the saying is. They did, however, avail to make more startling the intent visages and piercing eyes of those who sat near enough to them to have the light reflected from their faces. The large hall was filled with listeners of high intellectual quality. There was a total absence of the restlessness which had often made so embarrassing the addressing of an audience in Calcutta. Their dresses showed that they were almost exclusively Hindus and Muhammadans; only a handful of foreigners was mingled with the native crowd. The lecture was upon "The Reality of Mind" and was distinctly more technical than I ventured upon anywhere else in India, with the possible exception of Bombay. But it was listened to throughout—and it considerably overran the customary limit of an hour —without any sign of flagging attention, not to say, of willingness to leave the room. When I complimented Principal Richardson on the behavior of his students, many of whom were in the audience, he assured me that it was a part of college discipline not to permit a student to leave the room while the lecture was still in progress.

The most distinguished of our excursions during our stay in India was to Sarnath and Ramnagar, on invitation of the Maharaja of Benares. Of all places in Asia, and indeed for that matter in the whole world, Sarnath is one of the most interesting for the student of man's religious history. For here was the site of old Benares where Buddha taught, And of the various religions, Buddhism has commanded the adherence of the largest number of the human race; and of all others, in some important respects, it most resembles Christianity. The tradition is that after Gotama, by agonized contemplation under the sacred Bo tree, or tree of wisdom, had become clear in his own mind, a Buddha, an enlightened one, and so had attained to Nirvāna, he set out to proclaim this new way of salvation to his old teachers. Finding them dead, he determined to seek out and convert his five former disciples. An old hymn tells us how the Buddha, with his countenance glorified with his discovery, met on the way a wandering sophist with whom he had already been acquainted. The latter was so struck with Buddha's expression of religious exaltation and holy calm that he asked whose religion it was that could account for the happy change. "I am on my way now," replied the enlightened one, "to the city of Benares, to beat the drum of the Ambrosia (to set up the light of the doctrine of Nirvāna) in the darkness of the world." And on being questioned further as to his new doctrine, he responded: "Those indeed are conquerors who, as I have now, have conquered the three intoxications (the mental intoxication arising from ignorance, sensuality, or craving after future life). Evil dispositions have ceased in me; therefore is it that I am conqueror." Then the sophist answered: "In that case, venerable Gotama, your way lies yonder"; but he himself shook his head and turned in the opposite direction.

The direction which Buddha followed led him to the Deer-forest, where his five ascetic disciples were then living. And here, at the Deer-forest near Benares, the "Enlightened One" set up his school until he had converted about threescore of personal followers, or devoted disciples, and a certain larger number of outsiders who were more or less inclined toward his way of salvation. From here he made preaching excursions throughout Northern India, but never at a very great distance from Benares.

Chinese Buddhist pilgrims who visited Sarnath from the fourth century after Christ onward have left accounts of the Buddhist monastery centuries earlier founded there. One of them describes "the monastery of the Deer Park" as divided into eight parts, and surrounded by a wall within which were balustrades, two-storied palaces, a stupa of brick with a hundred rows of niches around it, each holding a statue of Buddha in embossed gold. West of the monastery was a tank in which, according to tradition, Buddha bathed; and to the West of that, another tank where he washed his monk's water-pot; and to the North a third where he washed his garments. There are still acres of mounds and excavations at Sarnath, which remain to show how extensive the monastery buildings must at one time have been. And besides very ancient tanks and stupas (or topes), there are Buddhist relic-towers in a good state of preservation at Sarnath.

As early as about seven o'clock in the morning the vehicle of the hospitable Maharaja drove up to the door ready to take us up to the spot where we were to cross the Ganges. The vehicle was an ancient and much dilapidated barouche; but it was accompanied and presided over by four servants dressed in faded liveries. Indeed, the driver had a large patch on a prominent place in his red coat. What, however, was there in such trifles to mar the comfort, pleasure, and improvement of the journey; or to lessen our gratitude for the thoughtful kindness which had made it possible?

When we reached a place in the river opposite the site of the Raja's ancestral palace at Ramnagar, we found a row-boat—or to use the more appropriate and imposing word, a royal barge—with five men waiting for our arrival. The fog on the Ganges was exceedingly thick that winter morning, about the thickest fresh-water fog I had ever seen. This made the row across the river extremely impressive for its exaggerated absence of all sights and sounds. All the senses could tell us was that we were on yellow water going somewhere enveloped in an impenetrable veil of mist. It was very weird and even awesome. One could easily imagine that one was being rowed by Charon's boatmen over the Styx to the "Land of Silence," even to the "Land of darkness and of the Shadow of death."

As we neared the other bank, after what seemed an extravagantly long period of river-passage, the mist began to thin out; and peering through it we saw a crowd of attendants and sightseers waiting for us, and in the midst a stately elephant caparisoned and properly officered for our conveyance to the place most sacred in the early history of the spread of Buddhism. The name of the elephant, we were told, was *Radhapiyari*, the "beloved of Radha,"—so called after the favorite mistress of the god Krishna. Radhapiyari, in spite of her exalted name and title to unsual pride, knelt for us most promptly and kindly; and we mounted as promptly and quietly as possible, for it is not well to keep an elephant whose name is associated with a god too long upon her knees. Mistresses of important personages, whether human or animal, are apt to have a nasty temper and an uncertain way of behaving themselves. And her lord and master Krishna was a god of many unscrupulous and mischievous tricks. Our much distinguished elephant waited, however, until we were well ready, and only signified its growing impatience by one or two insignificant snorts.

At the word of command Radhapiyari rose and started up the bank with an easy—for an elephant—and dignified pace. But when she had passed the place of her stabling, she seemed to become less pleased with the direction in which she was being driven, and less content with her load. Her frequent and persistent efforts to turn about, first to the right and then to the left, produced a curious corkscrew motion that threatened sea-sickness for the more sensitive of the four of her owner's guests who were seated on her back. Her impatience seemed to increase; small, short, but suggestive preliminary snorts gave token that the ending of this elephant-ride might not be altogether so pleasant as its beginning had been. We did not take kindly to the prospect of being run away with by an elephant, although she bore the name of the favorite mistress of the deity celebrated in the "song of the Blessed One." But the driver knew his beast; and the event showed the wisdom of firm and prompt treatment to one of Radhapiyari's temperament and sex. For, losing his own patience, he drew out his long steel prod and gave the beloved of Radha a most vicious stab behind the ear. The quieting, instead of exasperating—as I who sat next the driver feared it would be—effect of this punishment, was positively marvellous. From this time onward, the gait of her ladyship became less disturbingly serpentine; her expostulary snorting entirely ceased. When we reached the temple at Sarnath we rode once around it on the elephant's back, and then she went submissively down on her knees and to us, now safely conveyed and dismounted, held out to each one in turn, her trunk in petition of some reward. But alas and shame!—we had not thought to bring even a few pies worth of sweets, to say nothing of an apple from America or Japan. Notwithstanding such neglect, a tap of her forehead from her driver caused Radhapiyari's trunk to rise in *salaam*, to which we respectfully salaamed in return.

We then had opportunity to walk about the principal temple, or stupa, and examine it at our leisure more carefully. Briefly described, the structure consists of a stone basement 93 feet in diameter, solidly built by clamping the stone together with iron to the height of 43 feet. In each of the eight projecting faces of this lower part is a niche, which seems to have been intended to contain a figure of Buddha in his well-known sitting posture; and below the niches is a band of exquisitely sculptured ornament which encircles the monument. The blocks of stone covering the central part are carved in relief in a profusion of various forms, geometrical, animal, human, and representative of the Hindu gods —the whole so much resembling the mixture of Hindu and Western art employed upon the mosques we had seen in Delhi, that one could scarcely fail to believe both to be of substantially the same date. The roof is a modification of that prevalent with the Hindu temples both hereabouts and in Southern India. The detailed description of the other monuments and the disclosures of the excavations respecting this ancient seat of Buddhism, belong rather to the books on archæology than to our simple narrative of a winter's travel in India.

We returned from Sarnath in a much more modern barouche, which had followed us from the Raja's palace to the temple, stopping by the way to see one of his several gardens. On arriving at Ramnagar, the residence of the Maharaja of Benares, we were first of all shown the royal Bengal tiger; the beast, however, would not be provoked to anything more terrific than rolling over on his back, stretching wide open his jaws, and uttering a few angry growls. We were then shown through the palace; but since his Excellency was absent tiger-hunting and the library closed, we could not see its greatest treasure, the celebrated illuminated copy of the Rāmāyana. A row across the Ganges and a drive down its opposite bank brought us to our host's house in time for tiffin.

At 4:30 that afternoon I spoke in the hall of the Mission's high-school building on "Essential Christianity." The audience, both in numbers and in quality, was much inferior to that of the night before; and the embarrassment as to what should be appropriately said was increased by the fact that missionaries who had enjoyed in England a somewhat thorough theological training, and Hindu boys scarcely above the age of infants, made up a considerable portion of the audience.

An "At home," at which most of the guests were missionaries and their families, formed the last but not least pleasant of our experiences in the religious capital of India. From one of the guests, who was the son of a missionary but who was employed as a registrar in the government service, I heard for the first time about the incoming system of using "thumb-impressions" as a check to perjury and other forms of fraud. The willingness to commit perjury by denying their signatures was nearly universally prevalent among the natives of Benares and vicinity.

At the request of my host I spoke about missions in Japan; but stopped sooner than I should otherwise have done, for my hearers were becoming exceedingly nervous at the unusual mutters of thunder and the occasional flashes of lightning. And, indeed, there was good reason for such nervousness; for to be out in the night with native drivers and untrained horses, in a storm of thunder and lightning, involves no insignificant danger. The scene through the open door, as the guests were taking their carriages, was a very unusual and unusually wild one, for that part of the world, at that time of year. And when we were called at halfpast five next morning, to take the train away from "Holy Benares," it was still raining heavily.

CHAPTER IX

THE CAVES OF ELLORA

WE were now going from the ancient but still active and populous center of Hinduism, both of the vulgar and of the so-called "higher" sort, to the region where the three greater religions of India, and the political and social forces supporting them, had for centuries contended for the supremacy. In this region their successive triumphs over the religious consciousness of the people had recorded themselves in the form of monastic cells and temples cut out of the "everlasting hills" in enduring rock. In the way of structures designed for religious uses, it is difficult to conceive of a more striking contrast than that between the filth and tawdriness of the temples of Holy Benares and the solitariness and suggestive solemnity of the Caves of Ellora.

But we were also going from places where, in spite of a scarcity of food and some additional suffering on the part of that two hundred and thirty millions of the two hundred and thirty-one millions of the population of India who are always hungry, there were great rivers still flowing and few or none of the poorest were starving before your very eyes, and man could not help, to a region where the famine was most bitter, where cattle and human beings were lying dead or dying of starvation in the fields and by the roadsides; and where, on account of the numbers, efficient universal succor was practically impossible. (Lest the reader doubt this statement, let him give full credit to the story of the driver of one of the "water trains" on his way to one of the cantonments, who at a way-station was "held up" by scores of women begging "Sahib, just one drink of water before we die," and refusing to move out of the way of his engine until their petition had been granted. That train-load of water was emptied by the thirsty of the surrounding villages; and its pitiful train-crew went back to the source of supply for another load.)

It was, indeed, only on this excursion that we got a real taste of the bitterness of the famine of 1899-1901 in India. The foreigners, in general, and the well-to-do natives who dwelt in the cities, and even the half-starved crowds who still had strength enough left to walk or crawl into the cities, did not show to others, or themselves know by experience, the severest aspects of that terrible season. It was in the country, among the poorest agricultural classes (and the greater multitudes of India's population belong to these classes) that the horrors of such a famine became unmistakably clear—the horrors, and the helplessness in any satisfying degree of human agencies for immediate relief. It was, then, a valuable experience for us as travelers, if we were to understand and sympathize, to be subjected ourselves, though only for a day or two and in slight degree, under the stress of famine-hunger.

But we were also going from those parts of Northern and Northeastern India, where there was at the time comparatively little plague, back to the region of the Deccan and the plague-stricken Presidency of Bombay. And as it so happened, we were to hear on the way some concrete and authentic stories from one who had had much experience with that most terrific of pestilences, the "black death," the "great death," the bubonic plague. For when we changed to the through Bombay express at Mogul Serai, we were put into the same compartment with a young woman who, as it soon was made known to us, was a government nurse going home to England on her well-deserved furlough. From her my wife obtained by questioning many stories, modestly told by the brave woman, to illustrate, among other features, the freaky and incalculable way in which the plague often does its work of death. A high-caste Hindu woman, who was about to be confined, was brought into the hospital already afflicted with the pest. When her hour came, it seemed necessary to the nurses to summon a European doctor to assist her delivery with instruments. But her husband and other family friends refused and said that, although they much wished an heir, they would rather she and the child should both die, and the estate be forfeited to another branch of the family, than that she should be defiled by the slightest touch from any other man than a Hindu. Strangely enough, the gods justified and rewarded their fidelity; for the child survived and the mother recovered. In another case, a woman far gone with the plague was brought to the hospital, and refused to have her nursing child taken from her breast. There the infant clung, and in trying to satisfy its hunger, not only drew what nourishment it could from its dying mother, but even seized upon the poultice with which the mother's breast had been dressed. The mother died, but the infant took no harm. Sad indeed was the fate of the English nurse into whose open eye a delirious patient spat, as she bent over him in the effort to relieve his agony. The poor girl died within thirty-six hours.

There were several experiences which occurred on the way from Benares to the Caves of Ellora which left a distinct trail of suffering over the remainder of this winter in India. The night which I spent on the narrow shelf dignified with the title of an "upper berth," so filled my lungs with dust and cinders that it brought on an attack of pernicious influenza, from which it was impossible to recover until we had got to sea again. When the train reached Munmar Junction the next morning an hour late, we found letters which resulted in sending our native traveling companion on to Amednagar "with the luggage." *With the luggage* he went indeed; for he did not even leave the bundle of bedding, which was quite indispensable for our comfort in the bungalow of the Nizam of Hyderabad which His Excellency had placed at our disposal during our stay at the Caves of Ellora. However, we survived this and other slight inconveniences, and look back upon this part of our travels as among the most interesting and informing.

The Nizam of Hyderabad is the principal Muhammadan ruler of India. The family was founded by Asaf Jah, a distinguished Turcoman soldier of Aurangzeb, who was appointed in 1713 subahdar of the Deccan, with the title of "regulator of the state," but who rebelled and eventually threw off the control of the court at Delhi. This part of India continued to be what it had been for centuries before, the theatre of struggles between the Hindu and the Moslem rulers and the religions which they respectively protected and patronized. At the time of the Indian Mutiny in 1857 it was ruled by the father of the man who was Nizam at the time of our visit; and since he remained faithful to the English, his son had become established firmly as the principal independent native Muhammadan ruler upon the entire continent. Indeed, Hyderabad is the principal native state of India. The territory over which the

Nizam rules is rather more than 80,000 square miles, and is inhabited by nearly 12,000,000 of people. Its capital city is the fourth largest in India, and boasts approximately a half-million of inhabitants. On the whole, the present Nizam has been a wise and successful ruler. He was the originator of the Imperial Service troops which at that time formed the chief organization among the natives for the defence of India; and which in the present European war has rendered such hearty and efficient service to the cause of Great Britain and its Allies. Among his most recent improvements at that particular time was a railway which was to traverse a rich cotton country, and which on account of the abundant supply of cheap coal available could give low fares to the natives and yet afford a handsome revenue to the state. That very year of famine, 1899-1900, the total number of the Nizam's subjects receiving relief from his bounty rose to nearly a half-million daily. It was the railway just referred to which, although it was not yet finished through, we were to take in order to reach the point favored with such accommodation, nearest to our destination. The train which stood waiting for the belated Bombay express, on the track of the Hyderabad-Godavari railway, we boarded forthwith; and after some hours of jogging along over its recently built and therefore rough track, reached the station named Daulatabad from the world-renowned ancient ruined rock-fortress a short distance away.

At the station we were met by Dr. Ballantine of the American Board Mission, who had sent across country his tonga with its bullocks as draft-horses, and two servants in charge, to carry what of supplies of water, food, and bedding were necessary for us and for the animals. He had himself preceded the servants and the supplies on his wheel,—a much lighter and speedier vehicle than the tonga and the bullocks.

Our destination for the night was Rauza or Rosa, some eight miles from the station, near which was the Nizam's bungalow where the servants were to prepare our dinner and beds. It was necessary to rise very early the next morning so as to accomplish the somewhat difficult pedestrian task of walking to the Caves and substantially completing our superficial examination of them before the severer heat of middle and early afternoon came overhead.

The intending visitor to the only "caves" in all India which rival in interest the Caves of Ellora is advised by Murray's Hand-Book "to arrange for a bullock-cart with a change of bullocks on the road for each person of the party. Two persons in one cart will find it extremely uncomfortable. A traveler who does not know the language well must be accompanied by a servant or interpreter, and each person must have bedding and provisions." After seeing us ensconced in the bullock-cart, back to back with the driver's seat and facing to the rear so that the landscape opened to view only after it had been already traversed, Dr. Ballantine mounted his wheel, and directing the servants to follow in his tracks, soon disappeared in the distance. We did not, indeed, find the bullock-cart "extremely uncomfortable"; but neither, on the other hand, could it be called exactly comfortable. We did soon find, however, that, in view of the fact that neither we nor the servants were facile in the use of the language of the country (for in India there is no one native language which serves the purposes of easy communication in all parts) we had lost our guide and interpreter. Without him, our bullock-cart on the plains of the Deccan was not unlike a ship at sea without compass or pilot.

The bullocks were already pretty thoroughly used up by their long journey from home to the station at Daulatabad; and so they walked very slowly except when the shouting and gesticulating of the driver started them into a brief fit of ambling. The view from the highland to which we were now rising was very beautiful, especially as it began to be lighted up by a sun that had declined far toward its setting. The surrounding country is ordinarily deemed fertile, and is for that part of India thickly inhabited; although it now sustains only a fraction of its once teeming and thrifty population. Signs of the prevailing famine were by no means lacking by the way; indeed in spots they were only too obvious, abundant and frightful. Such signs were the bleaching bones of the animals which had already perished from lack of food and water; and the emaciated bodies of human beings wandering in the fields or lying by the roadside. Our way lay through two ruined villages,—Daulatabad, whose wonderful rock-fortress we were to visit on our return journey, and Rauza, the Kerbela, or holy shrine of the Deccan Mussulmans, distinguished as the burial-place of some of the most notable of the Mogul dynasty. Among them the most notable of all is no other than Aurangzeb, the rebellious and traitorous son of Shah Jehan. It was he who surrounded the city with a high stone wall with battlements and loopholes. But this, and the many mosques and tombs which abound in every direction on each side of the highway, are now largely in ruins. Rauza is still, however, a place of great resort by the Muhammadans in the summer months, on account of its mild climate; and nearby an annual fair is held in February, at which thousands of the faithful are accustomed to assemble for those mixed purposes of trade, gossip, and worship, which throughout the Orient bring the crowds together at all their festivals.

The slowness of our willing but tired beasts had now let the darkness overtake us; and the questions put to the few Muhammadans who stayed to be questioned, whether the foreign Sahib had passed that way, either elicited conflicting answers or no answer at all. It was becoming impossible to distinguish even the roadway from the upland plain over which we were taking no well-marked course, not to speak of steering the bullock-cart by the slender thread of a track left by the wheel of the bicycle. We seemed to be journeying over a trackless waste—somewhat up-hill, to be sure, but coming no whence and going no whither, and with no sign or voice to tell us of our destination or of the course which, even if it could be confidently followed, would surely bring us to the desired place. We could not communicate, either to suggest or to inquire, with any one who might be supposed to have the requisite knowledge. The situation was not really threatening,—or at least, I did not suppose that it was. But it did make a strong impression of unfamiliarity and weirdness upon the imagination. And perhaps the exhortation of the runaway Venetian boy who had such remarkable adventures and became so considerable a personage in India in the seventeenth century, was not entirely inapplicable to our situation at that later time. "I would warn the reader," says Niccolao Manucci, the so-called "Pepys of Mogul India," "never to stray far from his companions, because he might come across robbers in these woods. When they find any person apart from his company they rob him." But nothing of this sort was to be our fate; for, thanks to the suggestion of the feminine art of devising expedients, by making sure that the servant should frequently recover and verify the lost bicycle track with the light of a lantern, just as we had begun seriously to contemplate spending the night in the open air in the bullock-cart, we saw ahead of us the light of a candle set in the window of the bungalow.

A very good bungalow is that which the Nizam of Hyderabad has provided for his guests, from which to set forth to explore the caves of Ellora. On arrival there we found that another missionary friend was waiting for us,—Mr. Fairbanks having come across country, also on his wheel, to welcome us, and with us to have a first sight of the Caves of Ellora. It did not take the servants long to prepare a wholesome dinner; and since our friends had brought along an abundance of bedding for the entire party, we were in every way made comfortable. After dinner we tried faithfully to study again through Fergusson's account of the wonderful architectural structures which we were to see with our own eyes on the following morning; but unconquerable sleepiness soon overcame us, and we went early to bed. For the details of what we saw of these wonderful structures cut out of the solid rock, when regarded from the architectural point of view, we must refer the reader, some evening when he is not so sleepy as were we that evening, to Fergusson's *Rock-cut Temples of India.*

The Caves of Ellora are in several respects the best worth visiting of all the similar sights in the Continent of India. The Caves of Ajanta surpass them, indeed, in that they "furnish a history of Buddhist art, and illustrate the legends of the religion and the domestic life of the people from shortly after the reign of Asoka to shortly before the expulsion of the faith from India." The oldest of them is older than any of the Ellora caves; it is believed by some to date from about 200 B. C. The decoration of the Ajanta caves is on the whole more varied, rich, and beautiful. But the Caves of Ellora are much more accessible,—especially since the Nizam's railway has been built; they illustrate the religious symbolism and development of the Jain and Hindu, as well as the Buddhist, religions; and one of these temples, which is not only itself, but also has its court and immediate surroundings, all sculptured out of the solid rock, surpasses in size and magnificence, and in daring of conception and execution, anything else of its kind in that country, if not in the whole world.

To give an understanding of the gross features of this remarkable series of rock-cells and rock-temples we may be pardoned for quoting two official descriptions. "Architecturally," says Mr. Fergusson, "the Ellora Caves differ from those of Ajanta, in consequence of their being excavated in the sloping sides of a hill, and not in a nearly perpendicular cliff. From this formation of the ground almost all the caves at Ellora have courtyards in front of them. Frequently also an outer wall of rock, with an entrance through it, left standing, so that the caves are not generally seen from the outside at all, and a person might pass along their front without being aware of their existence, unless warned of the fact." "The Caves," writes Dr. Burgess, "are excavated in the face of a hill, or rather the scarp of a large plateau, and run nearly North and South for about one and a quarter miles. The scarp at each end of this interval throws out a horn toward the West. It is where the scarp at the South end begins to turn to the West that the earliest caves—a group of Buddhistic ones—are situated; and in the North horn is the Indra Sabha or Jain group, at the other extremity of the series. The ascent of the ghat passes up the South side of Kailas, the third temple of the Brahmanical group, and over the roof of the Das Avatar, the second of them. Sixteen caves lie to the South of Kailas, and nearly as many to the North, but the latter are scattered over a greater distance."

After a very early *chota hazri* we walked down the path of the sloping rocky hill, into and out of which the temples are cut, and began our tour of inspection at the oldest on the Buddhist end of the series. It being the season for one of the Muhammadan festivals following the close of the fast of Ramadan, we were not so much annoyed as is usually the case with professional, sturdy beggars. Even the man at the foot of the hill who collects fees from all the visitors in the name of the Nizam of Hyderabad was at first off duty attending the festival; but the bruit of our presence reached him in good time and he appeared with his visitor's book later in the day.

As has already been said, these monkish cells and temples hewn out of the rock in the sloping side of this cliff extend a full mile and a quarter from South to North, and with their chronological relation corresponding in the main to their locality, in the order of Buddhist, Hindu, and Jain. Of the Buddhist series the cave which bears the name *Dherwara* is the oldest and one of the most important; one other, the *Vishwakarma* or "Carpenter's Cave," is a parallelogram about 85 feet long, with a ribbed roof; and a third, the *Tin Tai*, is three stories in height. To me the most interesting thing in these oldest of the Buddhistic caves was the posture of the effigies of Buddha. He is not represented as seated in his customary posture but with both legs hanging down from the chair.

Of the Hindu series the most noteworthy, and indeed the most wonderful of all rock-temples, or even of architectural remains, in all India, is *Kailas*,—a structure at the sight of which one's amazement grows with every moment spent in its inspection. "It is not a mere interior chamber cut in the rock," says Mr. Fergusson, "but is a model of a complete temple such as might have been erected on the plain. In

MOST WONDERFUL OF ALL ROCK-TEMPLES

other words, the rock has been cut away externally as well as internally." Kailas is, then, an enormous monolith, a huge temple completely isolated from the surrounding rock of the hillside, itself made out of one unbroken piece of stone. From the solid rock surrounding this monolithic temple an enormous court has been excavated for it, which averages 154 ft. wide at the base, and is 276 ft. long at the level of the base, and with a scarp at the back 107 ft. high. On the outside of the curtain of rock which has been left in front of this court, are carved monstrous forms of Shiva and Vishnu and other Hindu gods; and several rooms are excavated inside its thickness. This rock-screen is pierced in the center by a passage which also has rooms excavated on either hand. The front portion of the court is somewhat lower than the main part; it has, however, two gigantic elephants cut out of the rock on the North and South sides. Ascending a few steps we enter the great hall of the temple, in front of which and connected with it by a bridge is a sheltered shrine for the sacred bull of Shiva, on either side of which stands a pillar of stone 45 ft. in height. Along the North side and rear of the court runs a series of excavations in two tiers with beautifully sculptured pillars. The outside as well as inside of this temple is profusely decorated with sculptures cut out of the huge monolith, or left as partly undercut pieces of the rocky hillside; and much of it shows signs of having originally been gaily painted. The Kailas is said to have been excavated about the eighth century by Raja Edu, who founded the town of Ellora, as a thank-offering for a cure effected by the waters of a spring near the place. It is dedicated to Shiva.

We had our breakfast that memorable morning sitting on the ground in the court of Kailas, or on the steps leading up to the temple. This finished, we made a more rapid survey of such of the other rock-temples as were most accessible, comprising some of the finest of the Jain temples at the extreme North end of the series. But the heat of the noontime sun became so overpowering that the rest of our tour of inspection was only very superficial. We reached the bungalow at the top of the hill pretty well spent, rested until 2:30, then had a hasty luncheon and took the tonga for the return journey to the station at Daulatabad.

The bullocks were much fresher than they had been the day before; the daylight enabled us to take an interest in the things by the wayside; and so the return-trip was really shorter, and seemed much shorter still, though in one way not so impressive as had been the journey of the night before, without guidance, over a trackless plain, in a darkness relieved only by the light of a single candle in a lantern. The fatigue and monotony of riding in a bullock-cart without springs were broken by two stops; one at the tomb of Aurangzeb where is enshrined part of the heart of this rascal, who probably did more than any one else by his base conduct to weaken and bring to a condition of decline the Empire founded by Akbar. Here we encountered a larger than usual crowd of sturdy beggars. The wheels of our friends easily escaped these nuisances; but the beggars had no difficulty in keeping up with the bullocks and the tonga. One big, well-fed lout of a fellow followed us for more than a half mile begging for a dole and eying us with threatening in his countenance. With him it was easier than usual to harden one's heart against the monotonous whine of "Sahib, backshish; Sahib, backshish."

The two cyclists went ahead and, in spite of the denials of the guards, obtained official permission for us to pay a flying visit to the fortress of Daulatabad. This fortress, like its neighboring temple of Kailas, is by way of a structure of solid rock, one of the wonders of the world. Out of the plain rises to the height of 500-600 ft. a huge conical rock of granite; and the sides of this have been scarped perpendicularly to the extent of from 80 to 120 ft. all around the base. Of the once populous and fortified city, there now remain only a few mean houses and huts, for the most part confined to the side of the rock nearest the road. At the bottom of the scarp is a ditch, before reaching which four lines of wall, including the outside wall of the city, had to be taken, and which when reached, could be crossed only by a stone causeway so narrow that it admitted only two men abreast. The sole means of reaching the top of the rock, where the palace and mosque and other princely buildings were situated, with the garrison and the munitions and stores which they required in case of attack, was through a narrow passage hewn in the solid stone. This passage is totally dark and winds around in the interior of the rock-fortress; and while at first it is high enough to allow one to stand erect, it becomes about half-way to where it comes out into the open, a steep stair, so low that one must crouch and so narrow that even a warrior ascending in single file could not draw his sword. To increase the unpleasant features of fighting one's way up this gallery, an iron grating was spread over the top of it in one place; and on this grating a huge fire could be kindled and kept up, fiercely burning, by the garrison above. While humiliating ourselves to reach the upper end of this passage, we could cherish the satisfaction of knowing that his Royal Highness, the Prince of Wales, and all the gaily dressed foreign and native ladies, and all the servants and the silver and the viands, in order to reach the palace on the top, had to go by the same painful and humbling route, when the Nizam of Hyderabad a few years before had entertained his distinguished foreign guests in this unconventional place. In spite of its seemingly impregnable character under all ancient and mediæval means of attack, the fortress of Daulatabad has several times passed between Hindu and Muhammadan hands.

When we arrived at the station we bade good-bye to our friends who were intending to bicycle home in the long moonlit night, and settled ourselves to waiting for the train which was expected to land us not very late at night at the Junction, where it was arranged that the early morning-express should pick up the car in which we were to lodge and take us on to Ahmednagar. We had no success in getting any supper, not to say dinner, at the station of Daulatabad. For although the station-master showed his willingness by opening the only storehouse of any kind of food the station contained,—a tin of biscuit, —the amount of other life being already in the way of appropriating the contents made us resolve that our own lives were not as yet in such immediate or prospective danger as to force us to share with the worms the remnants of the infested biscuit. Besides, we were assured that we should arrive at Munmar Junction before the station would be closed for the night and so in time for a hot supper. But this was not to be. For when our car, which was late in arriving at Daulatabad, had jogged along at the rate of ten miles an hour and we had reached the Junction only after midnight, we found the station dark and closed, the station-master afield somewhere in the large yard, and no one on hand who knew anything about the arrangements which had been made for our accommodation. We did, however, find a boy who undertook to guide us down the yard with a lantern, in the hope that we might discover for ourselves the car in which to find shelter for the remainder of the night. The walk was gloomy and even threatening enough; for it was between tracks and in a yard where the shunting of trains and single cars was constantly going on. Arrived at the spot where some empty passenger cars were standing, the boy then for the first time—native fashion—confessed that he did not at all *know* which of the cars had been allotted to us. He went to inquire, leaving us in the dark and with no very sure prospect of any shelter, not to say, "lying-down room," for the entire night. When he did return to identify the car belonging to the right train, it was discovered that the door next to us was locked and our guide had forgotten to bring the key. But we clambered over between cars and got in by the other door,—only to find that no light could be had until a messenger had been sent for a key to turn on the gas. At last, however, we could lie down in our clothes on the seats, take turn and turn about, trying to nap it and standing guard; but were prevented from sleeping much even when the turn came, by the hubbub of a busy railway-yard around us on every side,—until the time (6 A. M.) came for the morning through-express. Alas! we were again disappointed in obtaining the coveted morsels of food, for which we were getting more and more hungry. For instead of picking us up before breakfast and running us up to the station, where we could get a meal with the other passengers, they picked us up after the stop for breakfast for the other passengers had been made, and carried us off without any breakfast. Since we were now passing through "famine country," in the strictest and most terrific sense of the words, it was impossible by the way to procure anything to eat *(sic)* but a cup of tea without sugar or milk and a couple of shriveled oranges. There were more reasons than one, then, why we were glad to reach Ahmednagar, although not at all regretful that we had seen Daulatabad and the Caves of Ellora, or even that we had been brought into a condition of keener sympathy with the famine sufferers by going some thirty-odd hours without food, in the heat and dust of the Deccan.

CHAPTER X

AN OASIS IN THE DESERT

AHMEDNAGAR is the third city in size in the Deccan, having at the time of our visit somewhat more than 40,000 inhabitants; and although it has little or nothing in the way of architecture or other interesting objects to attract the foreign visitor, it is not without considerable historical interest. It was founded at the very close of the fifteenth century by Ahmad Nizam Shah Bahri, on the site of a more ancient city, Bhingar. The Portuguese pirates, who then ravaged a large part of the West Coast of India, for many years maintained friendly relations with Ahmednagar, so that they did not interfere with the extension of its ruler's power over a large surrounding territory, or with the growing prosperity of the city. But it fell into Akbar's hands in 1605, as the result of a celebrated siege in which figured Chand Bibi, the widow of Ali Adil Shah, whose story has been told in an English novel by Meadows Taylor, with the title "The Noble Queen." From this time on the city and territory of Ahmednagar was a possession contested by the Moslems, the Mahrattas, and the British, until the latter captured it under General Wellesley, afterwards Duke of Wellington, on the 12th of August, 1803. A tamarind tree under which the Duke is said to have taken his luncheon, is still pointed out on the South-west side of the Fort. Although Ahmednagar was afterward for a short time restored to the Mahrattas, it came finally into the possession of the British in 1817, since which time it has enjoyed such prosperity as the firm maintenance of order and respect for public justice can bestow.

This part of the Deccan is at best "a dry and thirsty land," the entire District being described as "a comparatively barren tract with a small rainfall"; and although the city is situated on a so-called river, the signs of universal distress from scarcity of water-supply were more obvious at Ahmednagar than at any other point which we visited during the winter. Just outside the city was a "famine-relief camp," where 9,000 human beings who could only be fitly described as scarcely "living skeletons," were collected for being fed sufficiently to keep them from a speedier death by starvation. Of these 7,000 were doing some work—for the most part by carrying small baskets of earth upon their heads—at building the embankments of an artificial lake which was to hold a three-year supply of water from the river Siva, on whose left bank the city stands, which could be stored in the seasons when the rains did their duty by way of supplying the river. The workmen and workwomen were housed in tents of straw open at both ends; but about 2,000 children and sick and feeble ones, quite unable to do any work, were cared for in a separate enclosure. The wages earned by those at work were, for the men from 1-8 to 2 annas, and for the women and children, 1 anna, 3 pies per day. But only the week before, our hosts, Dr. and Mrs. Robert Hume, had received from the United States nearly £7,000; and they will spend as much of this large sum as possible according to the same wise plan of helping those who can, among the starving people, still try to help themselves. It is the native character of the millions of India, with the exception of some of the Northern races and the comparatively few who, with the adoption of the Christian faith, have taken to themselves, together with reliance on God, its spirit of self-reliance, to lean heavily and even unscrupulously on any arm extended with the offer of assistance.

That sad winter the city and district of Ahmednagar had their full share of that other terror which was wasting the whole of that part of India,—the bubonic plague. As we drove back from our visit to the famine camp through the native city, the marks of its devastations were everywhere evident. The Autumn before the death-rate from plague had reached no fewer than seventy a day. But although Ahmednagar has a native population of 1,000 or more Christian converts openly connected with its Christian institutions, only two of this number had died of plague. The principal real causes of their escape were undoubtedly these three: innoculation against the plague, while refused by the Hindus on grounds of superstition, had been accepted by the native Christians under the influence and example of the missionaries; cleanliness of their persons, their homes, and their habits had already been in their lives substituted for heathenish filth, physical and moral; and their faith in God and in their foreign friends had kept them from all panic and had made them willing to obey orders and to follow good examples. All this, as a matter of course, was attributed by the more ignorant of their Hindu fellow townsmen, either to the goodness and power of the gods the Christians worshipped, or to the favoring craft of their protecting demons.

It was an inexpressible comfort to be again, after so long an interval, with home-friends and in a home modelled after the familiar New England type. A hot bath, and food and rest, a pleasant drive over the cantonment, and a good bed for the night, did much for the heartening of us both. I had, however, contracted a very severe and persistent influenza, and a threatening of the recurrence of intermittent fever,—evil companions which could not be shaken off during our stay in that climate and which threatened to wreck, but did not quite succeed in wrecking, all my plans for usefulness in Southern India and Ceylon.

The remainder of our altogether too brief stay in Ahmednagar was almost exclusively spent in getting acquainted with the work of the Christian Missions established there. And since this work seemed to be, on the whole, the most practically wise, effective among all classes, and organized in a thoroughly business-like way, with which we came into close contact anywhere, it may fitly serve as the occasion for one or two observations on missionary work in general, throughout India.

One of the most interesting and hopeful of the institutions of missionary enterprise on its side of active evangelizing was the "Second Church of Christ" in Ahmednagar, which is composed of converted low-caste Hindus; and which from the first has refused to receive any assistance from the outside, but has manfully and successfully struggled to sustain itself. As throwing light upon the work among the Brahmans I prized highly a long conversation with a Mr. N. V. Tilak, himself a converted Brahman, in which he gave me a most intelligent and sensible account of the present condition of Brahmanism among the Mahrattas. While still a Brahman, Mr. Tilak had reflected carefully, and had observed as widely as his condition afforded opportunity, with a view to discover elsewhere, or to devise for himself, some such reformed religion as should lift up his own people from their low estate. How low this estate had become, intellectually, socially and morally, my informant discussed with considerable detail. The picture he drew of the Brahmans, both high-caste and low-caste, was not flattering; but then it was no more damaging to Brahmanical character and its pride of caste than had been the picture drawn by the ascetic Raja of Benares. And Mr. Tilak's estimate of the social and family life of the Hindus was no lower than that which I had heard in Bombay from the lips of their sincere and well-informed Parsee friend, Mr. Malabari, or from the converted but sensible and sincere Brahman in Calcutta, Mr. Kali Banurji.

As a result of his meditations and observations Mr. Tilak had come to the conclusion that Christianity, as contrasted with Hinduism, even in the latter's most attractive speculative form and as held by the most thoughtful and moral of the high-caste Brahmans, commended itself especially in these three particulars: First and most important and fundamental of all, in respect of its clear and elevated and morally inspiring conception of God. I have already said that I have seldom or never met a thinker whose views on theology, in the narrowest meaning of that term (as doctrine of the divine attributes and divine relations to man) corresponded more nearly to my own, than those of Professor Bhandarkar of Bombay. But Professor Bhandarkar's views did not merely resemble in the most important ways the views of modern religious philosophy; they were substantially those views, and though views of a Brahman—or at least, of a thinker who had not declared himself a convert to Christian thought—none the less Christian monotheistic views, and not Brahmanical views at all. It is not to be denied, however, that all through the centuries of the development of Brahmanical philosophy there have been occasional thinkers who have in their conception of God come so close to Christian monotheism as to make it somewhat difficult to distinguish between the two. But these views, if they really have their origin in Brahmanical philosophy, almost always break down and lose their seemingly "clear and elevated and morally inspiring" character when they come to be tested by comparison with the Christian conception of *personal life.*

Mr. Tilak went on to mention, as the second great distinction between the higher Brahmanism and Christianity, the value which the latter sets on human personality, and the help which it renders in realizing the ideal of manhood. And, indeed, as we have already pointed out, it is a defective and morally misleading failure to conceive of God as perfect Ethical Spirit and Source of all personal righteousness, which constitutes the fundamental weakness of Brahmanical, and indeed, in general of Oriental religious philosophy. This failure has its inevitable effect in the undervaluation of the human person,—an effect which operates powerfully in shaping the constitution of civil government and the character of all the principal social relations. The individual human being does not count for much; because he is not regarded as intrinsically capable of developing that type of life, the personal life, which sums up within itself all that is of real value. In religion, the inspiring ideal of human personal life is to have it patterned after the Divine Life, the ideal of perfect Ethical Spirit, the struggle to attain, not a loss of the Self, or person, by absorption into God, but a moral likeness of the self-conscious, voluntary human personality to the perfect personal life of God.

The transition, so logically made by reflective thought, from a higher conception of the Divine Being to a more spiritual view of man's relations to that Being, was clearly apprehended by this converted Brahman. The second great superiority of Christianity to Brahmanism consisted in its improved doctrine of the Way of Salvation. Christianity conceived of sin as an ethical affair and as implying guilt which attached itself to the personal life of the sinner, and was indeed a manifestation of the character of that life; and it conceived of salvation as a moral and spiritual redemption of that guilty personal life. But Brahmanism regards sin as only the opposite of merit, and salvation as a ceremonial affair which, when complete, effects the extinction of selfhood by absorption into Deity.

Interesting, however, as was this exposition of the superiority, on grounds of reflective thinking, or as a matter of religious philosophy, of Christianity to the best of Brahmanical doctrine, from one who had left the latter to espouse the former, largely in view of the necessity for mental satisfaction; the sight of the practical results attained by the missionary work at Ahmednagar among the common people and low-caste Brahmans was even more interesting. That it might all be seen in the short time of our stop in the city, Dr. Hume had prepared a written program to which we adhered quite strictly.

On Sunday morning, after the conversation just narrated, visits were paid to the Sunday-schools of the two churches of the mission of the American Board. The school of the First Church had enrolled 612 members; it was supposed to be the largest native school of this sort in all India. Nearly all those enrolled are in attendance every Sunday; and there were all the signs of order, industry, attentiveness and genuine interest, which could be discovered in the best conducted of such gatherings in this country. The enrollment of the Sunday-school of the Second Church which, as has already been said, is composed of low-caste Brahmans and is wholly self-supporting, was at that time 125 members. The communicants in the First Church numbered 378;

the congregation was somewhat over 700, besides about 160 at the children's service. At 5 P. M. I spoke to an audience of more than 700, including a dozen or more Hindus—some of them Brahmans—on "The Essentials of Christianity." Nowhere else in India did I see such a native Christian congregation, or such evidences of vigorous native Christian life.

On Monday morning we started out in good season to inspect the school and other missionary institutions of Ahmednagar. The Theological Seminary was first visited, where 21 bright and earnest young men were in training for the native ministry. We next went to the High School and then to the Industrial School, taking its three sections in the order of carpentry, copper-beating, and rug-weaving. In the first of these sections 20 boys were receiving instruction in the making and repair of farm-implements and vehicles, and other of the common and universally demanded forms of native carpentry. In the next section 13 pupils were being taught one of the oldest and most distinctive of Indian arts, the art of beating copper into the forms of a great variety of useful and artistically decorated articles. But in the third section a large number, no fewer than one hundred in all—60 boys and 40 girls—were receiving expert instruction in another of India's oldest and most celebrated arts,—the art of rug-making. From the school we were conducted to the factory where 62 boys and 28 girls, graduates or advanced pupils in this art, were engaged in its practice. A Boston firm of dealers had contracted to take from this factory $100,000 worth of rugs annually, if so many could be made. (It should be said that since our visit, all these forms of industry have been greatly extended and others added, as important and integral parts of the missionary work at Ahmednagar.)

The inspection of the industrial side of the training given to the natives was followed by a return to the other sides of education. This included visits to the good-caste Hindu Girls' Day-School, where 54 pupils of this class were being taught; and later, to the low-caste Hindu Girls' Day-School, with its 65 pupils; to the Christian Girls' Boarding-School, which had at the time 157 boarding pupils and 118 day pupils; to the Bible Women's Training School, where 20 selected and mature native women were being trained as professional Bible-readers, so as to be fitted for access to Hindu Zenana women, especially those of the higher caste; to the Normal School, which had 76 in its Normal Department and 164 in its "model school," all of whom were being fitted to take charge of common-schools in the country districts—a form of education hitherto most neglected but, perhaps, of all others most important for the economic, moral and religious welfare of the millions of India; and, finally, to the Christian Boys'

Dormitory, which was housing 90 native youths in different stages of a Christian education. Besides all this, there was to be seen—though, of course, only in the most cursory way—the Mission Dispensary, the Mission Book-Depot, where in 1899, besides those judiciously given away, there had been sold Rs. 1683 of Bibles and other Christian books; the Brahman Gentleman's House; and the Chapin Home for Women, under whose roof 11 women and 7 orphan and friendless children were being cared for and instructed.

That Mrs. Ladd might see the Zenana work among high-caste Hindu women, a visit had been arranged for her to a private house where such work was going on; but, of course, to accompany her was totally tabued for any foreign man. I had my compensation, however, in being shown with an unexampled freedom the entire establishment of a middle-caste Hindu gentleman. The thoroughness of inspection permitted on this visit may be appreciated when it is understood that all the rooms, including those where the food was prepared, and even his wife's bedchamber, were thrown open. With much pride and perfect naïveté the owner displayed his gods, then drew the sliding-door in front of a narrow closet, on a shelf in which sat a Brahman in the customary attitude though not in the very act of worship. My host then explained that this priest was employed by him to come to the house and pray every morning from seven to ten o'clock. He was then, after having worshipped the sacred fire, given his breakfast with the family. "Leave of absence" was then allowed until the evening, when he was under contract to return and go through the appropriate ceremonies. "Thus," said the master of the house, "I employ and pay him to take entire charge of the religion of my family." The employee grinned acquiescently at this singular explanation in regard to the understood relations of the two. Whether the grin was discreditable, or otherwise, as compared to the feeling which the hired employee to do some one else's religion for him at a stipulated price and definitely fixed time would have expressed over an equally frank disclosure of the existing relations in this Christian land, I leave it to the reader to conjecture.

A garden-party given to us by the native Christians was appointed for five o'clock of the same afternoon. This had been entirely arranged by themselves and under the superintendence of no fewer than thirteen different committees. Perhaps, of all the things we saw at Ahmednagar to illustrate the benefits to India that might come from the transforming influences of a Christianity that took hold on all sides of human life, this, when one succeeded in realizing its full significance, was the most convincing. The English magistrate and his wife, and a number of missionary ladies connected with the Society for the Propagation of the Gospel,—including Miss Chubb, a graduate of Girton College,—were present as guests of the native Christians. The latter numbered nearly one thousand; and taken together, they seemed quite the most healthily happy gathering of natives which I saw in all India. Both boys and girls were playing native games,—the girls with all the modest freedom of movement and innocent joy in sport, which can characterize the English and American games of a generation ago; but which seem to be lacking to so much of what, in both these countries, is called "sport" in the present generation, with its craving for high-strung sensuous excitement. One of the boys' games was played in a diagram marked out on the ground and much resembling in every way the game of hop-scotch. Together with their native games, the girls by themselves played drop-the-handkerchief. During the festival we were once more crowned with garlands, as we had been the very first hour of our landing in Bombay by the native Christian young people there.

At dinner that day we met all the missionaries of the American board, and a few from other missionary organizations. Soon after the break-up at ten o'clock we took the night train for Madras; as far as the Junction at Dhond our accommodations were good, and we rested comfortably. But when, after a long wait at the Junction the train from Bombay arrived, we had our almost unfailing experience with the management of the government railways in India.

In spite of the fact of Dr. Hume's letter to the traffic manager, the guard claimed to know nothing of any reservation for us. He seemed inclined to pay no attention to providing the accommodations to which our tickets entitled us. But just as our insistence had won from him the offer to find something for the lady in the car exclusively reserved for women, leaving me to sit upright for the night, a young fellow who had sprawled over an entire compartment (the guard knew it very well) offered to move into the compartment where an acquaintance of his was in like manner sumptuously provided. Thus accommodated according to our rights, we slept so soundly that we were only awakened the next morning by a rapping on the car-door, which announced a friend sent forth to meet us, say "How d'ye do?" and bring us fine home-made gingersnaps for our *chota hazri.*

At the borders of the Madras Presidency we were forced to undergo a most thorough plague inspection, which was repeated a half-dozen times more before we were discharged at the city station. Because our tickets read from the Bombay Presidency, which was at that time very properly considered "infected" throughout, they were cut, and we were obliged to take out a "plague passport" which bound us under severe penalties to appear daily for ten days at the Municipal Office and get the proper officer's certificate of continued health.

There will be no better place than this to summarize briefly the impression received and deepened by every observation and experience regarding the work of religious reform in India. I have already said that the natives of India, including all the Hindu castes and Hindu races, are—we may say "by nature," since we know no other better way of expressing so original and fundamentally mysterious a fact—more religious than are the Teutonic or the Latin races. But as constituted and developed at the present time, it is doubtful whether they have either the intellectual or the moral vigor necessary to raise the standard of their religious doctrine or of the conduct of the practical life of religion, without help from the outside. On the whole, one's estimate of the Indian native character, of the sound and effective attainments of the more educated natives, of the validity and the value of the Hindu logic and the Hindu philosophy, and of the best outcome of the Hindu religion, as well as of the condition, socially, morally, and religiously of the multitudes, is apt to fall rather than rise with every week of added acquaintance with the facts. In my own case, I feel sure this experience has not been due to prejudice; for the initial impulses and expectations were quite in the other direction. I have been treated by the native leaders with quite unusual privileges, trusted more implicitly than it was fair to expect, and accorded distinguished courtesy. I have met many attractive and a few really noble native characters, who were not the product of imported Christian but, the rather, of intrinsic native influences. And yet, in general, I do not believe that Hinduism, whether orthodox or reformed, whether popular or esoteric, can ever raise or purify the native life of India, or even supply it with the necessary leaders in this work of uplifting and of purification. Hinduism has not the true and life-giving thoughts about God and Man, and man's relations to God and to his fellows, which are required for so tremendous a task. It has not the courage of its convictions, or the intelligent devotion to ideals that are at the same time high and pure, and also economically and socially practicable.

But, in the second place, the present educational system in vogue in India, both in the Government and in the missionary schools and colleges, is by no means the most economically defensible or fruitful of results. That a considerable number of the officials of the British Government in India had come to realize this, has already been pointed out; unfortunately the same thing did not seem to be true of an equally large number of the teachers and other officials in the missionary schools. To attempt to give the multitudes of the youth of any people an advanced education, in a language, literature, and by methods and text-books quite foreign to them, must always result in much waste and failure. Of the different experiments in this sort of "benevolent assimilation," Japan in Korea has thus far best escaped this mistake; but British India is still suffering from it to no small degree.

The attempt, then, so successfully begun at Ahmednagar, and now so much farther advanced than it was at the time of our visit, to train the natives to lead the life which the multitudes of the converted must live, in decent, courageous, self-reliant industry, because of faith in God and love of God and of their fellows, is as choice a gift as Christianity can impart. For, consider the case of the multitudes of India in their attitude toward the foreign and imparted religion of Christianity. "Rice Christians" by the hundreds of thousands of the lower orders of the native population can be gathered into the Christian community, in any time of famine. But if you had the conscience to gather them, where would you find the rice to feed them? And of what real use would it be to count their heads for report in the home-missionary periodical, if these heads could not be counted upon in their own land to work themselves free from the heathenish superstitions and filthy moral abominations of the popular Brahmanism? It is also quite possible to attract thousands of good-caste Hindus into your colleges, if you make the way into and through them easy, and are successful in getting the graduates into some coveted government position. But in four cases out of five, unless they, too, become in heart and life followers of the spirit that was in the "carpenter's son," it is better for your Christian college that these *babus* should not have its *imprimatur.*

And now consider the case of the much smaller number who are really, and more or less intelligently, dissatisfied with Hinduism, have lost faith in the Brahman, and are willing to defy him, break loose from Hinduism, and face the consequences of becoming, in heart and life and soul, followers of the religion of Jesus? What shall be done with and for them? This is a serious question. They will be outcasted. What that means for the poor, no one can form a picture who has not seen the phenomenon near at hand. The convert cannot expect a morsel of bread, a word of comfort, a bit of help, from any of his former relatives and friends. If he is willing to work, no one will give him work, will even allow him to work. If he is a cook, he cannot cook for Hindus. If he is a blacksmith, he cannot shoe a Hindu's animal. If he is a wheelwright, he cannot mend the cart of a Hindu farmer. Life is incomparably easy for the Jew who is cast out of the synagogue in this country—if, indeed, that thing is ever done to those who have means of self-support—compared with the Hindu who is outcasted in India. This, then, is where such Christian work of industrial education as was being done at Ahmednagar is needed throughout the entire continent on the grandest scale, in behalf of the religious reform of India.

When some man of what we count wealth in America gives several millions to found and carry to self-support a Christian industrial village in India, we shall have a model for the transforming influences of a practical Christianity operative on a continental scale.

But India is being raised toward a Christian philosophy, a Christian morality, a Christian civilization. Much of this process—perhaps most of it—is indirect and outside of the fold of baptized converts. There are many things in Indian character and Indian philosophy, and a few things even in Indian popular religion, that are helpful accessories, approachable sides, points of attachment, for the work of religious reform in India. Of all the obstacles to this most desirable result, however, so much bad example in the doings of so-called Christian nations is by far the greatest, most obstructive and difficult to overcome.

CHAPTER XI

MADRAS AND FORT GEORGE

WHEN we arrived on time at the city station of Madras, although it was only a little past six o'clock in the morning, we found Dr. Skinner, Acting President of the Christian College, waiting to welcome us. We were at once captivated by the physical aspects of this capital of Southern India; for, although it has not the imposing situation or stately collection of public buildings of Bombay, or the variety of educational, civil, and commercial interests of which Calcutta can boast, it has, much more than either of the other capitals, the charm of the tropics as we had already fallen in love with it in Colombo and Singapore. This first favorable impression was deepened when, in the afternoon of the same day, we took the drive along the beautiful red road (the *Marina*) extending from the Fort, over the Napier Bridge, past the Senate House, the Presidency College, and other public buildings, by a sea, the waters of which have that deep and brilliant blue that cannot be matched in temperate or northern zones. And, besides, much of the way the driveway is overhung by mighty banyan trees which form a veritable tunnel and furnish an agreeable coolness even under the tropical sun.

Another class of physical phenomena, quite as interesting but not quite as agreeable, gave notice that night of our having arrived in a somewhat different zone. For I was awakened out of a sound sleep by my bed shaking. My first thought was of a train of cars passing near by. But no train of cars could shake a house of this solid structure in this fashion; for the bed was swaying in the "billowy" way which characterizes the most vicious kind of earthquakes. (It should be explained to those who have not been initiated to the same variety of experience, that the shakings which the earth gives herself when she decides that it is time to ease the pressure by changing her levels underneath you, are seldom or never precisely alike.) Yes, it was a real live earthquake, and rather the most severe I have ever experienced, in spite of several decided shocks during my visits to Japan. One of the household, and he a man of science, when he heard the grinding of the walls in the tower where he slept, ran out into the verandah expecting the building to fall. The papers next day reported the earthquake as widely extended through that part of India.

The ten days of quarantine, during which a daily visit to the health-office and an inspection by one of its doctors were prescribed, threatened to be something more than a temporary nuisance. For the influenza which I had contracted on the cars from Benares was in the feverish stage, and made me so weak and miserable that during the period of quarantine it was necessary to lounge or lie in bed all day, in order to get up for the afternoon lecture and the evening social function. But rarely good luck was in store for us in this regard. For the examining surgeon was an Eurasian: and after we had gone to him for two days, he said it was more fitting to our dignity that he should come to us. The medical member of the Faculty of the Christian College gave us two excellent pieces of advice, one social, the other physiological. The government doctor, said our wise friend, being an Eurasian, will on no account offer to shake hands with you. Do not you offer to shake hands with him. Then he will have no chance by feeling to detect that you have a fever. If now, he went on to say, "I give you some medicine, you will be well in two weeks; if you do not take any medicine, you will be well in a fortnight." I refrained from shaking hands with the Eurasian doctor and from receiving medicine from the European doctor;—and in due time reaped the reward of both kinds of abstinence.

The lectures in Madras were of a peculiar, and in some respects superior, interest to those given in either of the other Presidency cities. The average audiences numbered some four or five hundred, and consisted chiefly of graduates and older students of the different colleges, almost exclusively Hindus so far as the native part was concerned, but with a considerable number of Europeans who were almost without exception Christian. In his introduction Justice Shephard, then the chief magistrate of this Presidency, referred to the "curious connection" between Madras and Yale, in that this University had derived its name and £800 of endowment from Elihu Yale, who, when he left the country after being Governor here, took away with him "a bag of diamonds."

After the lecture, Dr. Miller, who had been for many years the successful and beloved President of the Christian College, rose, and in the fluent way which the natives so much enjoy, spoke some good words about the lecturer, and then went on to commend the goodness of Justice Shephard in the matter of arranging for the course. Then again the Justice spoke, explaining that the course was virtually under University auspices, although it could not be given in the Senate House, since this building was now being got ready for an art exhibition. In his closing sentences the Vice-Chancellor became somewhat tangled up, and sat down leaving one of his periods in mid air, as it were.

The colleges and schools and educational institutions generally of Madras are neither so numerous nor of so high average grade as are those of either Bombay or Calcutta. But they have some very interesting peculiarities. Perhaps the chief of these are due to the fact that there are almost no Muhammadans or Parsees to be found among their patrons or their pupils; while the type of Hinduism prevalent and to be encountered in various practical ways, in Southern differs from that of Northern India. The Madras Christian College is, however, probably the best equipped and best managed of all the similar collegiate institutions in the country. Its collegiate department had at the time of our visit about five-hundred in attendance. The preparatory school had not yet been made up for the ensuing collegiate year, owing to the unfortunate fact that the proofs of some of the examination-papers had been stolen from the registrar's waste-basket into which he had carelessly thrown them. The school, however, ordinarily numbers as many as one thousand. One of the most interesting facts connected with the organization of this institution is this;—namely, that almost all the boys in one of the hostels of the College come from a body of Syrian Christians, who form a community of fully 400,000 members on the Western Coast not far to the South of Goa. My informant thought that the time of their settlement in India was lost in antiquity; but they seem to have antedated the Portuguese Roman-Catholics by a long period of time. They have suffered much persecution in past years, especially by the Portuguese Catholics; and some have become adherents of the faith of their persecutors. But the greater number still remain adherents of the Patriarch of Antioch; though there is a difference of opinion which divides them into two sects. One sect holds that the Patriarch has the absolute right to the appointment over them of their clergy; the other sect holds that he has only the right to confirm the choice of their congregations. These Syrian Christians are said to be a much more vigorous and reputable people than the converts of Portuguese Catholicism. As judged by their racial characteristics they are evidently the descendants of some body of Syrians, who migrated here and intermarried with the natives.

Subsequently we paid a visit to the Northwick Girl's Boarding School, which was then under the auspices of the Free Church of Scotland. These girls were all Christians; and their rather shy and dull demeanor, in contrast with the bright and "up-and-coming" manners of the Hindu girls whom we visited in the afternoon of the same day, disclosed plainly the fact that the former came from families of low origin and bucolic surroundings, and the latter from good or high-caste Brahman families. This school is, however, doing excellent work in educating Christian teachers for the lower grade schools and wives for the Christian boys,—a very important and laudable species of manufacture.

At the Chetty School for Hindu Girls we saw another exhibition of native jugglery and snake-charming. Strange that both these exhibitions should be given for our entertainment by schools for girls! But here were 300 bright black "tots," who seemed keenly to appreciate the tricks and the jokes of the juggler. The cobra produced from under the cloth was rather too lively to allow me, who sat well within his striking distance when it was allowed to creep to the edge of the table, to enjoy to the full the juggler's tricks; I was not at all sorry when the venomous reptile was safely boxed up again; though in general, I am not particularly afraid of snakes, but rather am pleased to watch their maneuverings and changes of temper. Of course, the jokes of the juggler could not be appreciated by the two foreign guests who were not at all acquainted with the language in which they were uttered.

The foolish and degrading superstitions, the filthy and licentious and cruel practices, and the generally low intellectual and moral tone of the popular Hinduism, are even more conspicuous and unmistakable in Southern than in Northern India. Probably the same thing is true of the inefficiency and untrustworthiness of the natives in all manner of domestic, civil and commercial relations. In all these respects the testimony of the foreigners who had lived longest with them and who were their most affectionate and sympathetic friends coincided with my own observations. The reasons for this difference seem to be chiefly the following four: The mixture of races in the North, especially of the Indo-Aryan stock, is markedly superior to that of the South; something —it is impossible to say just how much—is due to the influences upon the physical organism and the habits of living, particularly as affecting the sexual relations, of the more distinctly tropical climate; the Muhammadan rule, in spite of all the corruption and criminal procedure of the different rulers of the Mogul Empire, was on the whole an improvement upon that of the native Hindu princes and of the Brahmanical priests and courtiers; and the foreign governmental and religious influences, especially those flowing from the British East India Company and Portuguese Roman Catholicism, in the earlier days, tended to provoke and exploit rather than to improve and restrain some of the worst of the native characteristics, both public and private.

One who had come from Japan so recently could not be long in Southern India without noticing the characteristic difference in the temper of the two peoples as evinced by the differences in the very sounds which filled the air. In Tokyo we had lived for six weeks just over the fence from a large public-school; in Madras our bedroom and dressing-rooms were just across the narrowest lane from two sides of the school-rooms of one of the colleges. In Japan not a cross or disagreeable noise came from the building or the playground of the school to our ears during our entire stay. The songs and pleasant cries of the children at play, the low and cheerful words of instruction and command from the teachers, were the only sounds which were to be heard from the compound of the school. Even the crows in the grove farther away seemed to be only gently expostulating with us for occasionally appearing on a landscape which they had come to consider peculiarly their own. But from the playground of the school in Madras came only high-pitched, shrill-voiced noises, usually of wrangling and quarrelling, though the disputants never came to blows. Scarcely an hour of the day passed when our ears were not disturbed with the noises of some row going on in the school-room itself between the boys and their native teachers. Looking through the blinds to see what could be the matter, one would behold the pedagogue gesticulating and orating against idleness, or insolence, and hear him threatening all sorts of punishment, none of which seemed ever to be applied. One would hear the pupil "sassing back," and see the other pupils grinning at the sport, occasionally taking part themselves in the game of verbal bluster,—of course, usually on the boy's side. And anon, another order of noises arises from the lane below the window. This time it is a man and an old woman who are abusing and threatening each other, with a small crowd of idlers looking on. But it all ends in gabble. Even the crows have the most exasperating of caws, and they are ceaselessly at it.

They are certainly the originals of the species *corvus impudens.* I have seen them come down upon the maiden who was carrying around the plate of cakes at afternoon tea and carry off a piece as plunder. One must guard one's skull from a possible fracture in this way, who takes a meal in the open air.

But when we are told of the two Brahman policemen who tried to extort Rs. 5 from a set of moneylenders, more than thirty in number, and failing in their first efforts, invoking the name of the law broke into their club-house and placed cards and other gambling implements in hiding, that they might subsequently discover them, we are not entitled to be quite so much amazed at such *heathenish* dishonesty as we should be if somewhat similar occurrences had not been known to take place in our own Christian cities. The *dhobee* or low-caste Hindu who does your washing, will let out your evening dress to an Eurasian man or woman to be married in; the driver of your carriage when you go shopping expects his fee from the shop-keeper for bringing him a customer; if you want approximately pure milk, you must have the cow milked in the sight of a trustworthy witness, and even then the milker may be practicing adulteration by having a bottle literally "up his sleeve," from which a concealed rubber tube makes connection with the pail; your cook will kill your own chickens and charge you the full market-price for them on his bill; and various other similar annoyances will afflict your life in Southern India. But all these things have their parallels in America; and after all, Southern India is a most delightful place to live in, if only one has the income for a good style of upkeep in foreign fashion and can flee to the hills in the worst of the tropical heat.

The annoyances of which a few selected specimens have just been rehearsed are trivialities. Not such are some other abominations with which the British Government does not venture actively to interfere. While in Madras I received a visit from delegates of the Hindu Reform Association of Travancore. This Association was then moving for the abolition of child-marriages; for the re-marriage of widows in order that these unfortunate women might be saved from compulsory prostitution; and for the increased purity and temperance of the young men. But in Travancore the Brahmans, now as ever, are so much in the ascendency that the Maharaja himself is compelled to be annually weighed in a scale against an equal weight of coin (it used to be gold, but it is now a mixture of silver and copper), and the entire sum distributed to the Brahmans as a bribe to prevent their intriguing against his rule. Only the oldest son of a Brahman family marries; the younger sons consort with the girls of the warrior caste; and in Travancore the warrior caste has no legal marriage whatever. My informants considered the British Government needlessly conservative and timid about reform, fearing, apparently, the disturbance of their revenues by any sort of agitation. They instanced, in proof, the case where, when the native ruler and his Ministers were ready to change the law which disinherited all Christians, the Government under the influence of the Travancore Brahmans discouraged all efforts at this reform.

No one who has looked the facts in the face with an observing eye can place the slightest confidence in the attempts, current even with some writers upon the subject in this country, to explain away or to "spiritualize" the atrocious indecencies and gross licentiousness, not only permitted but prescribed and actually practiced by the Hindu worship in Southern India. The doings at many of the festivals, the prevalent decorations of the temple walls and of the cars used in the religious processions, and many other evidences, are in plain contradiction of the more tolerant view. To quote again from an authority on the religions of India (Prof. E. W. Hopkins) when speaking of the "esoteric side" of the sectarian religions: "Obscenity is the soul of this cult. Bestiality equalled only by the orgies of the Indic savages among the hill-tribes is the form of this religion. . . . . A description of the different rites would be to re-duplicate an account of indecencies, of which the least vile is too esoteric to sketch faithfully." Extermination, root and branch, by the criminal law is the only sound policy in dealing with such pretence of "freedom of religious worship."

It was pertinent to this state of things, as well as

a significant revelation of them, that while we were in Madras a discussion was going on in the newspapers as to the right of the Government, not only to proscribe, but also to prescribe, text-books for instruction in the schools and colleges of the Presidency. On looking up the matter I came upon the following extract from the civil and penal code. It dealt with an exception to the general law and ran about as follows: "Except that the law shall *not* apply to indecent and obscene representations of sacred personages." Now, undoubtedly, it may be claimed that certain models of Greek art and stories of the Greek gods, and even certain passages of the Old Testament, would seem to need a similar exception in their favor. Let us grant this, but without expressing an opinion as to whether such exceptions ought to be made, or not. The admission would not on the whole destroy the truth that no other mixture of nastiness with religion, which is apt to meet in any way the eyes of the observing traveller as he journeys round the world, is on the whole quite so disturbing and repulsive as that sure to be met with in the popular and traditional worship of Hinduism in Southern India.

One cannot see intelligently the City of Madras, not to say understand with some thoroughness its present condition and history in the past, without knowing something more than a hurried visit can bestow about the celebrated fortress called after the name of the patron saint of those who built and defended it, "Fort St. George." We were particularly fortunate in receiving an invitation to breakfast from the chaplain at the Fort at that time, the Rev. Mr. Penny. After breakfast it was planned that we should inspect the place and learn something of its history and of the most notable of the men who have been in the past connected with it, from Mrs. Penny who has since added to her other published works a history of Fort George that is the standard authority on the subject.

The founding of a fort, which it is supposed was called "Fort George" for the reason, in addition to the appropriateness of the name as applied to any similar construction by the British, because it was completed on St. George's day (April 23) was nearly contemporaneous with the founding of Madras. From the beginning, the Fort and the City, and indeed the entire Presidency, have gone through similar vicissitudes. The whole enterprise dates from 1640 when Francis Day, chief of the East India Company's settlement, obtained a grant of land for the present site of the city from a native ruler. The condition and policy of the Company, its relations to the Rulers of the Mogul Empire, and the dangers which constantly threatened both these foundations, are all told in such an amusing and vivid way by the Italian adventurer, Manucci, the so-called "Pepys of Mogul India," that it is well worth while to quote a somewhat lengthy passage from his narrative descriptive of a somewhat later time. In January, 1701, the Mogul General Dā-ud Khan had been sent to the Province of the Karnatik by Aurangzeb, to look after the interests of the Empire. He had encamped in front of the great fortress of Arkat, "an ancient strong place of the Hindu kings." The Mogul General, says Manucci, was in "the greatest imaginable fury and passion," because the presents which the English had sent him were so insignificant in comparison with his importance; and he was threatening at once to despatch an armed force against Madras and Fort George, and then to follow it up by going in person with a large army. Thus would he let the English know that he was a person of much more importance than they had reckoned him to be.

Manucci was much distressed, for he was friendly to all Europeans and also on good terms with Dā-ud Khan; besides, he foresaw that his own interest would be seriously imperiled by the spreading of such a strife over that entire region. He therefore paid the Mogul General a friendly visit, bearing—as the custom is even to this day throughout the Orient—presents in his hand. Manucci confesses that he did not lead the conversation to the point desired, until he had made it "easy" by putting his interlocutor into "high spirits" by getting him to drink—follower of Muhammad though he was—"copiously of the European wines that I had brought for him."

But now let the wily Italian Christian tell in his own words how he for the time circumvented the plans of the wily Muhammadan man of war. Manucci opened his plea with the subject which was really of most importance to both parties. "As concerned the revenues," says he, "I pointed out to him that when the English came and occupied Madras it was nothing but one vast plain full of sand, uninhabited and without any name or fame in India. On the other hand, it should be remembered that it was now highly populous, full of active merchants and other residents. It was the money of the English and their good government that had created all that prosperity, coupled with the justice they administered to everybody without fear or favor. If he intended to act with so much harshness and injustice, all the nations of Europe would abandon India. He must recollect the income and benefits which Aurangzeb had acquired; for from what entered and left Madras alone, he collected more than one-hundred thousand *patacas* (equal to about $70,000 in gold at the present time). In addition, there were many merchants, weavers, cloth-printers and others, for all of whom the English provided a livelihood."

After summing-up the much larger sums which were earned by the subjects of Aurangzeb through the mercantile and manufacturing enterprises of the English, Manucci goes on to urge Dā-ud Khan to remember that "the whole of this remained in the country, and in exchange for this the English carried off to Europe no more than some cotton-cloth. Let him reflect that if he objected to the residence of the English in Madras, and if he bothered his head about their gaining such considerable sums, it was requisite for Aurangzeb and his subjects to give them time to withdraw to Europe. They (the English) set little store by the place; yet if they were forced to abandon it, they would also give up the other towns and factories they held in the Indies. In that case they would cease to be friends and become enemies. Upon their departure they would without fail seize every ship they came across, and thereby spread ruin and desolation throughout the Mogul Empire."

The Mogul General yielded to the entreaties of Manucci, who afterwards chronicles his visit to Fort George, and the compliments and civilities between him and the English Governor, Mr. Pitt. After being saluted with guns, whose salvos at first terrified him, dined and wined, and enriched with more valuable presents, some of which were of his own choosing, Dā-ud Khan went back to his own camp in better humor. But this reconciliation lasted only a brief time; for in 1702 the Mogul blockaded the town for several weeks, but retired without capturing it. Forty years later, however, it was bombarded and captured by the French; was restored to the English by the Treaty of Aix-la-Chapelle; was invested again by the French but relieved by the timely arrival of the English fleet; was threatened by Hyder Ali's horsemen in 1780; but since then Fort George has remained in English hands free from external attack.

We spent our first hour and more in the Church of the Fort, which was built in 1680 and is therefore the oldest building used by the Church of England in all India. It is well kept up and is in most excellent condition. The chunam work here is all of ground shell beautifully polished. The gallery, where the Governor and his Council used to sit in state, but where now the prisoners of the Fort-prison are seated when they attend service under guard, is supported on beautifully carved wooden pillars; its railing is also of the same carved wood-work. The carving follows Hindu patterns, such as one familiar with the Hindu temples would quickly recognize. But the posts of the railing are a curious mixture of Hindu and Christian symbolic figures. They are quadrangular in shape; at the base are two carved elephants whose trunks are elongated and turned upwards, with carved birds on top, and the whole crowned with cherubs. All this work is beautifully done.

A large picture of the last-supper, which was formerly placed back of the altar, is now hung on the wall over the front arch of the sanctuary. The story has been spread abroad that this picture is "loot" from the Portuguese Cathedral at Pondicherry. But our host assured us that this could not be; since the picture is catalogued among the treasures of the Church at Fort George, before Pondicherry was taken. On the side-walls and columns of the Church are memorials to a number of men celebrated in Anglo-Indian history. Some of this work is in marble sculptured by such artists as Bacon and Flaxman, in their finest style. For in the gallery of this Church have sat at public worship several of the most celebrated men in the history of the British Empire;—among them Wellington, Clive, Cornwallis, and other much respected and beloved, though not so widely known men, like Munro and Hobart, who have acted as Governors of Madras. Among the memorial tablets is one to the missionary Schwartz; it was erected by the East India Company, because of his distinguished services in procuring and keeping peaceful relations with the native princes. The Raja of Mysore so trusted and loved this good missionary that at his death he placed his son under the tutorial care of the good Christian Schwarz.

Twice the Church of Fort St. George has been used as a granary and horses stabled in it in times of siege by the French. Once a portion of its rear tower was knocked down by a cannon ball. Its roof, however, was built so as to be for that day bombproof. Outside are the tomb-stones of some of the more notable men of the Presidency,—merchants and others; and among them are the names of several families such as Fleetwood, Morse, Titus Oates (nephew of the more celebrated man by that name) who were obnoxious to the Government of Charles II, and who were therefore sent as a good riddance to India for positions there.

On returning to the house we were shown the Church plate, one piece of which, the salver to receive the offerings, was the gift of Governor Elihu Yale. The proofs of Mrs. Penny's forthcoming book were also kindly offered for our inspection; as well as, also, such of the records on the foundation of which the book was written as I cared to see. Among these was the notice of Yale's marriage to the widow Hinmers, or Hynmers, whose husband had died the May before. This notice was as follows:

> Elihu Yale and Catherine Hinmers, relict of Joseph Hinmers, were married by the Rev^{d} Mr. Richd Portman minister, given in marriage by the Right Worshipfull Stringham Masters Esqr, Gov^{n} Henry Oxe^{n} den & John Wilcox Bridemen, Catherine Barker & Tryphena Ord Bridesmaids.

Almost precisely the same date (1686) Manucci married a Roman-Catholic widow who was the daughter of an English magistrate named Christopher Hartley, by a Spanish woman. In his diary he is careful to state that she was "legitimate," and how much he mourned her loss when she died just twenty years later. During most of this period Manucci lived at Madras, "or Fort George"—the two titles being deemed identical—and practiced ceremonial "blood-letting" and other forms of the medical art, to his own great profit and with distinguished success. He has left a curious account of this "royal blood-letting," how it was done, and what happened to him on such occasions. "Ordinarily the princes and princesses have themselves bled twice in the Month of March, and the interval between the two bleedings does not exceed twenty-four hours. The operation is begun half an hour before the setting of the sun. Three days afterward they take a purge; but if necessity demands a shorter interval they do not wait the three days, but are governed by the requirements of the case. In the month of September the same procedure is repeated." The same quaint chronicler has left us much information as to the intrigues and quarrels between the Hindu Brahmans and the "Roman Brahmans," as the Portuguese priests found it expedient to call themselves; as to the struggles of the British East India Company with the Mogul officials, the French, and the Portuguese; and as to other strange occurrences and adventures within and around the city of Madras and the Fort St. George.

We further paid our respects to the memory of "Old Eli" by visiting the tomb of his infant son. It stands back of the Law School building and is of very curious structure. The tablets, or rather inscriptions, are cut in the stone face of either side of an archway which runs through under the monument. On one side is the memorial in old English to a Mr. Hinmers, Madame Yale's first husband; on the other side the memorial to the Governor's infant son.

The places and institutions connected with the history of French and Portuguese Catholicism in Madras are scarcely, if at all, less interesting than those of the English occupation. Recognizing this, we were driven one day after tea to the Church of

Saint Thomé, where the priest acting as prior in the absence of his superior showed us every courtesy. In the center of the new cathedral some ten or twelve feet below the pavement is the grave of Saint Thomas, the patron saint of the cathedral and, indeed, of all this movement of Roman Catholicism in Southern India. The prior then ordered the sacristan to show us the vestments of the bishop,—a Portuguese ecclesiastic, under whom is the cathedral and its parish, but who is not subject to the archbishop of Madras. Some of these vestments were embroidered in Madras, and others—as I understood the priest—"at home," that is, in Portugal. The relics were carefully wrapped in parchment, or paper, and inscribed with the names of St. Thomas, St. Francis Xavier, St. Elisabeth, and a number of martyrs. They had been authenticated and sealed by some old-time bishop and were enclosed under glass in a silver-gilt reliquary. But the padre did not know what the relics were, or when they were sealed up, or anything about their history.

I took advantage of a holiday to visit in the companionship of one of the foreign teachers most learned in such subjects, St. Thomas Mount, otherwise known as the Great Mount. In one place Manucci speaks of his "house at the Big Mount." This hill is some seven miles from the Fort, but at its base is the cantonment which used to be the headquarters of the Madras Artillery. The Mount is a knoll of greenstone and syenite about 300 feet high, crowned by a very old Armenian Church. We went by cars to the station, but there procured a funny little bandy into which one crawled through a door in the rear, and then sat half-curled up; and in this way reached the foot of the Mount. From the railway on the left we had seen Little St. Thomas, and a fine long stone bridge, over which pilgrims used to pass in great numbers, on the way to visit this sacred place. The bridge was built by Armenian merchants when they were numerous and wealthy in Madras and vicinity.

The ascent to the Church on the top of the Great Mount is by a flight of one-hundred and twenty-one stone steps. Near the foot of this lofty stairway are inserted into the pavement two tombstones, one of which bears the date of 1604 and the uncommonly unconventional but frank and suggestive statement in Latin that the person beneath was *filia prima legitima* of her father, but *filia naturalis* of another and more advanced number.

On the top of the Mount are the remains of a fortification, with embrasures used for guns and three cannon used for signals; besides, there is a building once used as a flag-station from which the mail steamer approaching the harbor used to be signalled. Here also are the ancient church and a building inhabited by priests. The church was built, according to the sacristan in 1544, partly at the side of, and partly around, a yet more ancient structure of small stone and chunam work, the date of the erection of which is lost in antiquity. This more ancient part of the structure is used both as a sort of vestry and as a storeroom. From the small alcove in the tiny dark room—so we were assured—was taken a stone carving of a cross and a dove, which my learned companion identified as similar to others that go back to the 7th century A.D. The alcove is now occupied by American lamps and cans of kerosene. Extremely curious paintings in oil representing the twelve apostles hang high up on the walls of this ancient church; and just in front of the altar is a painting of the madonna and child which the sacristan boldly attributed to St. Luke! What food for reflection is there not for us in the facts that centuries before Christianity was taken to our heathenish and barbarian ancestors, the now despised priests of Portugal and the cruelly afflicted and harrowed Armenians had spread their form of Christian truth and ritual widely over all of Southern India?

Wishing to remove the suspicions which I learned that the Roman-Catholic Archbishop Colghan, quite unlike the Jesuit Fathers in Bombay, entertained toward me and my work, I called upon him that we might be better acquainted with each other's views. The Archbishop had at that time been in Madras for fifty-six years, returning only twice in all that time to the home-land. He came down at once into the reception-room on my card being sent up. He was at first rather coolly quizzical and skeptical as to my intentions with "the heathen," or as to the possibility of my making any impression upon them. But when I explained my purpose as connected with the hope of doing something to resist the incoming tide of agnosticism and atheism among the present generation of *babus*, and said that I considered this a worse condition in its relation to Christianity than their Hinduism, he agreed with me. In the course of our conversation the Archbishop quoted the saying not long since of Lady Duff, who had declared that soon all India would become either Catholic or agnostic. I did not dispute the statement, though I could not agree with it. When we parted, the attitude of the Archbishop had become entirely cordial, and he gave me his official blessing.

We were also particularly favored with a chance to see other interesting things of a quite different order, by an invitation from Dr. Thurston, the custodian of the Madras Museum, which is perhaps the most interesting in all India, to take breakfast with him and then under his guidance see the things most worth seeing in the collections under his charge. The things which are most interesting are the oldest authentic relics of Buddhism. In this museum are the celebrated marbles which were taken from an exceedingly old Buddhist place on the river Krishna, but which bear plain marks of Greek influence, and, it is not unlikely, were done under the supervision and according to the plans of some Greek artist. Here also is the oldest authenticated relic of any sort in all the world. It consists of three tiny chips of bone, enclosed in a small casket of beryl with a gold-capped stopper, and a rim of beaten gold to seal it on. We do not know that these are bits of Buddha's bones; but we do know that they were considered such as early as the date of King Asoka, 240 B.C. For the whole relic as enclosed in its box of beryl was taken from the center of a large and hitherto undisturbed stone casket bearing authentic inscriptions of that date. The Buddhist priests of Burmah or of Kandy, Ceylon, said Mr. Thurston, would give thousands of rupees to any thief who would steal that relic and convey it to them. And there are thousands of thieves in Southern India who would willingly undertake the job if they could do so with any hope of success. But the incomparable treasure is closely watched.

Among the other interesting objects in the Museum at Madras are many old brasses taken from temples and elsewhere, and illustrating the earlier art-work of Buddhism,—especially an elaborate candelabrum with a very spirited figure of a dancing Siva in bronze. Of another order is the wooden cage in which Captain Arbuthnot was confined for seven months during the Chinese war of 1840-42. A melancholy interest attached to the skin of a cobra kept in a large jar of alcohol, because its former occupant had fifteen years ago killed Dr. Thurston's cook, who stepped on the snake as he entered the cook-house in the dark.

Dr. Thurston had the same story to tell of the untrustworthy character of not only his house-servants, but also of his assistants in the Museum; and also of the impossibility, except in rare instances, of training this untrustworthiness out of them. And, indeed, it only disappears when a quite radical change is effected in the underlying motives and views of life, by the introduction in the center of the personal life of religious convictions and principles. How shall a man be much better at heart than the god he worships, however he may be restrained by conventional and legal considerations? But we have probably already said enough upon this important point.

During our entire stay in Madras we were entertained with that delightful hospitality which, without fuss or formality, makes one feel thoroughly welcome and at home. We were all the time meeting with incidents and with persons to throw side-lights on the character of the life led in Southern India by the cultivated and the ignorant, by the rich and the poor, of both the native and the foreign population. At a dinner given by Justice Shephard, whose house was situated about a mile beyond the cathedral of St. Thomé and had for its nearest neighbor our widely known theosophist countryman, Col. Olcott, we met a score or more of ladies and gentlemen belonging to the official class. The *menu* here had for the dessert a very unusual stimulant. For after the ladies had retired to the drawing-room and the men were about finishing smoking and talking around the table, our host, addressing the custodian of the Museum who was an authority on the subject said: "Thurston, step out here and see what kind of a snake this is which my boys killed on the compound near the house this afternoon." We all went through the doors that opened upon a brick-paved verandah only a step or two above the level of the ground, and there stood three turbaned men holding up by three strings—one at the middle, one at the tail, and one at the head—a reptile of very respectable size and length. "It is a tic-polonga, or Russel's viper," said this authority on snakes, the moment he set eyes upon it. Now I had learned at the "zoo" in Madras, where one of the most famous collections of poisonous snakes is on exhibition, that the tic-polonga is rather more to be shunned and dreaded than is his rival, the cobra. For the boy, who was anxious to increase his fees by exhibiting his skill in handling poisonous snakes, wanted more annas for entering the glass cage where were kept the largest of the tic-polongas, than for venturing among the cobras. He got his fee from us; but not for risking his life among either den of reptiles with deadly fangs and uncertain tempers.

Another most interesting and improving dinner-party was the one at which I met ten or twelve of a Synod of English Wesleyan missionaries whose stations were in the country surrounding the city of Madras. One of these gentlemen told me the story of his experiences in the native state of Mysore, which, after having been taken over by the English, was restored to the hereditary Raja, after he had been well educated under carefully selected English tutors. As a result, the state of Mysore was being exceedingly well governed. On the other hand, another missionary told of the Prince of Arcot, who is kept in or near Madras and away from his people; but is being pensioned at the rate of Rs. 10,000 a month by the British Government. Several thousand of the Muhammadans belonging to the former retinue of this native prince were also being liberally pensioned. My informant regarded this as being, even if necessary, a monstrous evil and intolerable burden for the people of India, who have to support this system of pensioning Hindu and Muhammadan princes. All this confirmed my opinion that a paternal native government, under supervision and by carefully trained and selected native officials, must be the best solution available for a long time to come, for such cases as the native states of India, for the Philippines, and for Korea.

During the latter part of the stay in Madras we

were the guests of Mr. and Mrs. Pittendrigh, in whose house Dr. Miller and Rev. Mr. Weston—both most agreeable and kindly companions—were living at the time. Their compound and its mansion were of a sort to be found only in the tropics where Europeans have settled for a long time, and so have learned how best to adapt their ideas of sanitary and comfortable living to the rigorous conditions imposed by climate, native customs, and the limitations coupled with the luxuriousness of available supplies of service, food, furnishings, and other household expenses. This was one of those very large old compounds, shaded with tropical foliage, and a commodious and solidly built old house (our room was fully forty feet in length) which in spite of the fact that you may occasionally find a scorpion in your shoe or a cobra on your front stairs, and always have to fight the destruction of all wood-work by the white ants, has no superior for contributing to the joy of just living and doing your modicum of the daily tasks.

Besides the regular course of lectures at the Christian College of Madras, but under the auspices of the Madras University, I gave a number of other conferences, talks, and public addresses, before different kinds of audiences,—but all of them exhibiting in their attention and in their questions a high degree of intelligence and interest. Of these one of the very best was composed of one hundred members of the "Teachers' Guild," to whom I spoke on "American Universities." The magnificence of the sums expended in buildings and equipment in this country amazed my audience; but were I compelled to speak again on the same subject before the same audience, I fear that the obligations of truthfulness would require an even less favorable account of the net result in scholarship and character of all this vast expenditure.

The day of the last lecture came, on the morrow of which we were to leave Madras and go still farther southward on our way back to Ceylon. The audience was larger and more enthusiastic than at any time before. After the lecture was finished, two natives—one a Christian-College man who was in the civil service, and the other a prominent Hindu barrister—moved and seconded a vote of thanks which was carried with much show of enthusiasm. But the most interesting and encouraging result of the work in Madras was the fact that both of these speakers, and the majority of the audience, seemed to comprehend and sympathize with, in a truly astonishing way, what it had been the half-suppressed but deeper purpose of the lectures to accomplish.

We left Madras on the last day of winter, with the thermometer standing every day well up around the nineties, and somewhat worn out with the entire winter's experiences. But we bade farewell with sincere regret to the group of friends who came to the station to see us off. We were to share the compartment with a Lutheran missionary and his wife, who were on their way to Colombo to take the steamer Oldenburg to return to the United States. And although I found my upper berth too narrow for a perfectly safe lodgement, I did not tumble out until we pulled into the station at Madura.

CHAPTER XII

MADURA AND SOUTHERN INDIA

THE city of Madura, although it has neither the size nor the attractions of the three Presidency cities and is comparatively rarely visited by the foreign tourist, is nevertheless, when fairly judged by its history and its local interests, "no mean city." It was the capital of the old Pandyan dynasty, which continued its dynastic rule for a far longer period than is granted to most forms of government; for it held sway over all this part of India from the 5th century B.C. to the end of the 11th century A.D. The last of the old Pandyan kings showed the vigor of his Hindu ancestors by exterminating the Jains and conquering the neighboring kingdom of Chola. But the power of the Mogul Empire was creeping or storming farther southward, and the king of Madura was himself overthrown by an invader from the North. After a Moslem army had held the Hindus of the city and district in subjection for a period of years, the province passed again under Hindu rule. In the middle of the sixteenth century its governor, Viswanath, established the so-called Nayak

Dynasty. It was the greatest of this line whose military exploits are recorded in the correspondence of the Jesuit missionaries; who adorned Madura with its temples and public buildings; and who extended his empire widely over the adjoining districts. In 1736 the District fell into the hands of the nawab of the Karnatik, and the line of the Nayaks was extinguished. Twenty years later the English took charge of Madura in the alleged trust for a Muhammadan prince. But he was the last independent native ruler of the Karnatik; for his son ceded his rights of sovereignty to the British East India Company in 1801. From the history of Madura learn in brief the history of all of Southern India.

At the station we were met by Mr. Chandler who took us to the mission-compound of the American Board where we had breakfast and a brief rest. As soon as the fiercest midday heat had somewhat subsided, or rather as soon as the sun was not quite so much overhead and so able to execute its most direct and mortal strokes, we visited the schools in the compound, had tea, and then at five o'clock went to the church near by where a "welcome service," native fashion, was to be held. This consisted of prayer , the singing of Tamil lyrics, the reading of a printed address in English by one of the native teachers, and the presentation of a palm-leaf manuscript in Tamil. This manuscript I at first took for an ancient treasure; but it was soon discovered to be a very modern affair. It had just been prepared in imitation of original antiques by some of the native caligraphists and contained the address of welcome, the Lord's Prayer, and a variety of other things. It was designed for deposit in the Yale University Library. After these welcome exercises I made a brief response.

The Brahmans of good caste in Madura were the most conspicuously "liberal" in their intercourse with the missionaries and other Christians of good social standing, of any men of their class whom we meet during our travels in India. They had given generously to a hospital which was conducted without interference from them under Christian auspices; and they had co-operated cordially in a street-preaching campaign against intemperance. The Hindu Club which was formed chiefly by these Brahman gentlemen invited us and our hosts—not omitting the ladies—to take afternoon tea on their grounds in the suburbs of the city, where we were politely served in the open air near the tennis-court. So faithful to their temperance principles are the gentlemen of the Hindu Club that they do not allow drink of any kind except tea to be served on its premises,—not even soda-water in bottles; in order, as they explained, to avoid suspicion and even "the seeming of evil." Instead, everything in our entertainment was carried on in a fashion not to be distinguished from the most strictly Pharisaical of

Christian gatherings,—with one exception however. The Brahmans did not drink tea with us or serve even the ladies of our party by pouring and passing tea for them. To do this would have been to break caste. But if there are to be lines drawn in the name of religion between friends and social equals, of a ceremonial character, what fault can Christian sects find with these Brahman gentlemen? One must draw the line somewhere; if it is once for all granted that any line of this character is anywhere to be drawn. And to break the bread of social communion with those who had no caste standing was to render oneself justly liable to excommunication. Yet, when on the following evening I spoke concerning "the Conception of God most in accord with Science and Philosophy" to an audience which crowded the hall of the Young Men's Christian Association, a native Hindu Judge presided, and these high-caste Brahmans were of the most intelligent and appreciative of the audience.

In the evening of this first day in Madura I told to the weekly gathering of the missionaries of the region at the house of our host my observations in Japan. For, as there has been occasion to remark before, all classes in India were then especially interested in the impressive spectacle of the rapid changes and advances in civilization afforded by this Far-Eastern nation, and in its probable influence as a stirring example for all the other Oriental peoples.

The next morning we drove to Passumalia, stopping on the way to visit the palace of Tirumala Nayak and the mission-schools in that quarter of Madura. This palace seemed to us one of the most interesting sights of its kind in all Southern India. The prince who was its builder was one of the greatest rulers of the District of Madura,—"the greatest of all in modern times," he has been called—and his rule lasted gloriously for nearly forty years. The palace itself has been restored by the English so thoroughly that it is now one of the finest public buildings in all India. Some of its halls, when in their original perfection of finish and decoration must have been truly magnificent. What was the throne-room, a court under the Grand Dome, is 61 feet in diameter and 73 feet high. There are four holes in the middle of the roof of the room, 54 feet high, which was Tirumala's bedchamber. I quote the legend that "Tirumala's cot was suspended from hooks fixed in the four holes, and that the large hole between the two holes on the southern side of the room was made by a thief who descended by the chain suspending that corner of the cot and stole the crown jewels. Tirumala is said to have offered an hereditary estate to the thief, if he would restore the jewels, adding that no questions would be asked. On recovering the jewels, he kept his word, but ordered the man to be decapitated!" The British now use the building as a *palais de justice;* but as their custom too often is, they have shown an utter indifference to all æsthetical considerations by cutting off all the beautiful vistas on all sides of the court, and fencing off the offices with dirty and ragged screens set up between the pillars. It is no insignificant remnant of barbarism, or slight handicap of the most cordial relations, for the governing race to show this kind of indifference to the subtler feeling of the governed.

At Passumalia we were shown over the different branches of a thoroughly well organized and highly successful missionary work; after which I spoke to the whole body of students and teachers, some 500 in number, in their large hall. The singing was extremely interesting, especially a Tamil lyric with a violin accompaniment and the rhythm strongly marked by striking together a small pair of cymbals. The *tempo* seemed to me as strictly as possible seven equal notes to the measure, rather than a sequence of four and three. The effect was very peculiar and made one feel as though one must spring to one's feet and sway one's body and dance in truly heathenish fashion. It was easy to see how such music could work a multitude of singers into a kind of frenzy. And, indeed, we did see how such an effect was actually attained when we witnessed an exhibition given on shipboard by a band of devil-dancers who were on their way to the Paris Exposition of 1900.

At breakfast there was rather a warm discussion over the best way of educating the natives, during which it became apparent that Southern India is not afflicted to the same extent as Bengal with a superfluity of *babus*.

After returning to Madura in the almost intolerable sunshine and taking a brief rest we visited the "Great Temple," the most beautiful portions of which as it now stands were built by this same Tirumala Nayak who built the great palace already described. This famous structure forms a parallelogram of 847 feet by 729 feet, surrounded by nine *gopuras*. (pyramidal towers) over the temple gateways and constructed in the Dravidian style, of which the largest is 152 feet high. With its grounds this enormous temple covers thirteen acres and is exceedingly wealthy in revenue and resources. As being one of the finest of its type, and the only other ones approaching it in size and—albeit somewhat tawdry—magnificence, not situated near enough our route to be visited, it merits a brief description. The entire *Great Temple* of Madura really consists of two parts, or temples, one on the East dedicated to *Minakshi*, "the fish-eyed goddess" who was one of the consorts of Shiva, and the other to the god Shiva himself, the member of the Hindu Trinity who represents "the ascetic, dark, awful, bloody side" of the Hindu religion. The worship of the Shivaites here and elsewhere in India is always tending toward what is most beastly and cruel and lustful in the most degraded conceivable forms of religious cult. The entrance to Minakshi's temple is by a gate and through a painted corridor about thirty feet long, which is called the Hall of the Eight Lakshmis, from eight statues of the goddess by that name, which form the supports of the roof on either side. This corridor is used freely as a bazaar by various sorts of traders and money-changers. The temple itself is a maze of corridors and rooms used for various purposes opening off from them, with rows of elaborately carved pillars on either side. Some of the capitals of the pillars are formed with a curved plantain-flower as a bracket,—a fashion which is found elsewhere in the Dravidian temple architecture. By some this is called "the Hindu cornucopia." One of these corridors is 166 feet long and runs up against a large door of brass that has stands to hold a multitude of lamps which at night furnish it with "a dim religious light."

The number of bazaars in this temple is amazing and the revenue from them is, as we have already indicated, very large. One interesting trick for increasing this revenue in other ways than by the profits from the bazaars is to make public announcement that the goddess, to whom the temple is dedicated, will be taken out of her special room some night at eleven o'clock and conveyed to the bed-chamber of the god. A great crowd gathers and pays liberally to see the marriage ceremony. But something unpropitious, such as the sneezing of a

Brahman, occurs to prevent the completion of the ceremony; and so another paying festival of the sort can be proclaimed for the following year.

At this temple some of the most degrading practices of the popular Hinduism, such as the prostitution of the Nautch girls and the seduction of women by the priests are still kept up pretty much as in the earlier times; and there is the same lack of any sort of religious feeling which was to be noted under similar surroundings at Benares. In both these positive and negative ways the popular Hinduism in India is greatly inferior to the popular Buddhism in Japan.

We had an amusing experience with the sacred elephants of the Great Temple of Madura. At first, one of them was introduced by his keeper as ready to perform for us in consideration of suitable *backshish;* but he failed utterly to earn his money by doing any tricks, not even picking up the two-anna bit thrown down on the ground before him. But no sooner was it known that foreign sahibs, willing and able to pay well for such entertainment, were touring the temple—and the news of it seemed to diffuse itself everywhere almost instantaneously—when all the other elephants kept appearing athwart our path, and began without entering into any preliminary negotiations or efforts at a contract to show themselves off. One of them, a huge she-elephant, was most amusing. She trumpeted, she danced, she hopped about on three legs, and all in fine style. She received her well-merited fee, which she promptly and dexterously picked up from the ground.

Near the temple is a tank, almost as celebrated and elaborate in its way as is the temple itself. It is called the "Tank of the Golden Lilies." In the center of an island surrounded by the waters of the Great Tank stands a picturesque temple. There is a chamber in the tank built by the queen Mangammal, who according to tradition was seized and starved to death by her subjects about 1796 A.D. These cruel rebels, while starving, also tortured their queen by placing food so close to her that she could see and smell but was unable to reach it. A statue of her Brahman lover may be seen on the West side of the Tank; and on the ceiling there is the portrait of the paramour opposite the portrait of his royal mistress. Two sides of the wall of this corridor are somewhat gaudily painted with representations of some of the most famous pagodas of India. On one side is a belfry with an American bell of good tone. Of the twelve pillars sculptured on the sides of the corridor, six represent a strange monster called *Yali*, the conventionalized lion of the South of India.

The most interesting feature of the Great Temple taken in its broadest expanse is the *Hall of a Thousand Pillars*. As a matter of fact, the number is said to count up only 997, many of which are hidden from view, since the intervals between them have

THE TANK OF THE GOLDEN LILIES

been bricked up to form granaries for the pagoda. It is not, however, the number but the marvelously elaborate nature of the carvings which makes this Hall with its one thousand pillars so famous. Its builder, who was Minister of the Founder of the dynasty, is represented near the entrance seated like a skillful rider on a rearing horse. But perhaps the most noteworthy of all is the building called Tirumala's *Choultrie*, the New Gallery dedicated to the presiding deity of the place, who was fabled to pay the ruler a visit of ten days annually. This hall has four rows of pillars supporting a flat roof. Tirumala is distinguished by having a canopy over him; and on his left is his wife, the Princess of Tanjore.

This extravagance of size and riot of decoration in the use of mythical forms, animal and divine, are especially characteristic of the temples and pagodas of Southern India. To the student of anthropology, of comparative religion, and of the history of social evolution, Southern India offers some of his most complicated and difficult problems. The peoples and their family of languages, which are divided into not fewer than a dozen more or less closely related dialects of which Tamil and Telegu are spoken by the greatest number, are designated "Dravidian," a term derived from the Sanskrit. They are a dark-skinned race, and, so far as can be known with any assurance, they are the *aborigines* in the strictest sense of the word, of all the southern part of the continent and extending over into the northern half of the island of Ceylon. The nearer we come to their aboriginal condition, the more isolated from all other peoples, in their physical characteristics, their customs, and their language, do the Dravidian peoples appear. But as the fair-skinned, more intelligent and highly developed Aryans extended their conquests and their superior type of living to the southward, they overruled but mixed with the dark-skinned and relatively wild and savage Dravidians. That happened which always happens; the superior race modified but did not wholly destroy the characteristics of the inferior race. When Portuguese and French and Dutch and English were for two hundred years contending for supremacy in trade, in possession of territory and influence over the native rulers, and even for success in the propagation of their favored forms of religion, the process of modification went on apace. It is going on at the present time. But it has never been complete. There are today tribes of naked savages living in trees, worshippers of the cobra who regard this snake as the ancestor of the tribe and look upon it as their totem, and appoint groves for its habitation, where it is fed at the public expense and has its established shrines, and practicers of all manner of strange and grossly heathenish customs, among the descendants of the original dwellers in "the medley of forest-clad ranges, terraced plateaus, and undulating plains," which stretches across this part of India. But on this very account, Southern India has a certain fascination due to its weirdness and uncanny nature that is lacking to most of Northern India. Among the Dravidian peoples, the popular Hinduism, too, is of all places most bestial and grossly licentious, as has already been said. The same fact will be further put in evidence when we come to describe our brief visits in Ceylon, where devil-worship is an affliction into which the converts to Christianity even down to the third and fourth generations may not infrequently suffer a relapse. And yet that is true of the dark-skinned Dravidians, which is true of the dark-skinned races generally, they are capable of developing some very amiable traits and of receiving a good degree of intellectual and æsthetical development.

On the morning of March 3d I made an address—the fifth within forty-eight hours—to the native pastors of Madura and the vicinity, and then we took the eleven o'clock train for Tuticorin. The heat was something frightful, the thermometer standing at above one hundred in the railway car. A visitor to Tuticorin in the sixteenth century mentions its fame as the center for pearl fisheries. At that time the fishers and divers were mostly native Christians. But because of the deepening of the channel these banks no longer produce pearl-oysters in remunerative quantities; but "chank-shells" are still found here and exported to Bengal.

The anchorage at Tuticorin is no less than five miles from the shore; but by paying what seemed rather an exorbitant fee for "embarkation," we reached the little steamer "Hindu" in fairly comfortable fashion. It turned out, however, that there were only five cabins in the entire ship; these were not nearly enough to accommodate the number of first-class passengers booked for this trip. The number of this class was much greater than usual, since a homeward-bound steamer was sailing the following day from Colombo. "The lady" was therefore sent to one of the cabins allotted to the somewhat miscellaneous crowd of her sex, and I was assigned to the same cabin with the Bishop of Madagascar. This right-reverend gentleman, however, while disclaiming all personal prejudice against me, insisted that he must have his secretary with him and wanted the captain to order me and my luggage moved out. To this I did not give a ready assent; although I, too, had no personal prejudice against Portuguese or French or any other nationality of bishops. But the affair settled itself in the most amicable and satisfactory manner. For it was found that the berths were much to narrow to accommodate a person of such corporal, not to say ecclesiastical, proportions, as the Bishop of Madagascar; and so a tent was erected on the upper deck and within it cots set up for the Bishop and his secretary, while I was left sole occupant of a two-berth cabin; for it proved too late to call back my wife.

The terrors of the passage on account of rough water were nought; but the discomforts of landing at Colombo were considerable. We were kept waiting so long by the quarantine doctor who, before he would release the first-cabin passengers, inspected in such a thoroughly leisurely way (I cannot say with how much medical thoroughness) the several hundred coolies on board the "Hindu," that the friendly host who had come out to meet us with a boat was obliged to go off without his guests. We hailed a sampan, however, and were fairly pitched into it with all of our luggage except one piece, a Gladstone bag. One of the coolies in another sampan had grabbed and made off with this,—a species of black-mail which an appeal to a police-man, when we had reached the jetty, prevented the rascal from making profitable. The customs-officer did not even ask us to open our trunks or bags; thus before long we had secured a garry and a bullock-cart and were on our rather lengthy journey to the house of the missionary where we had been entertained on our visit to Ceylon four months before. But since two missionaries of his Board were occupying the accommodations of the house until they could take Monday's steamer for England, and since the Galle Face Hotel was full, and far away, Mr. Tarrant, of the firm of forwarding and commission merchants, Tarrant, Henderson & Co., who then lived at "Temple Trees," a bungalow near by, kindly offered to take us in for Sunday night. Our adventures that night and subsequently belong to the next and concluding chapter.

CHAPTER XIII

CEYLON AND HOMEWARD-BOUND

IN geological formation, climate, social and religious customs and institutions, and in civil and political history, the Island of Ceylon is closely related to Southern India. The aborigines, or at least the inhabitants for untold ages previous to authentic history, were probably the ancestors of a tribe of hunters who still inhabit some of the eastern jungles. The great Hindu epic, *Ramayana*, tells how its hero Rama conquered part of the island and took the capital of its king. It is doubtful, however, whether this boast of Hinduism represents the truth of history. Buddhism, which still shares with the popular Hinduism and the most superstitious forms of devil-worship the allegiance of the lower orders of the people, was early and more permanently planted in Ceylon. Its conversion to Buddhism at the beginning of the third century is still marked by the multiplication of the *daghobas*, or curious bell-shaped reliquaries of solid stone, and the monasteries, which meet the eye of the foreign tourist on every hand. After the expulsion of the religion of Sakya Muni from India by the revived power of Hinduism, Ceylon became the principal seat of the southern and most degraded type of this great reformer's religion. It remains in this position to the present day; and this fact gives it a peculiar interest to the student of comparative religion.

The Singhalese rulers of Ceylon and their followers, and the Tamil rulers of South India and their followers, fought and invaded each other's dominions back and forth through several centuries. The Portuguese, Dutch, and British trade-interests contended for economic supremacy there in scarcely less determined and unscrupulous fashion. The Portuguese in Ceylon, as everywhere else, treated the native rulers in such overbearing and tyrannical fashion as to make themselves particularly obnoxious. When the island was conquered by the forces of the East India Company it was at first made a part of the Company's south-Indian jurisdiction, and administered from Madras. But by a convention entered into with the Kandyan chiefs in March, 1815, the complete sovereignty of Ceylon passed into the hands of the British, who guaranteed the inhabitants civil and religious liberty, and who there, as everywhere, unlike the Portuguese and their modern imitators in the management of colonies, have been so wise and liberal in their administration that no serious disturbance of the public order has occurred since.

The well-known missionary hymn says of "Ceylon's

isle" that "every prospect pleases." But let us quote the more expansive and rhetorical description of Sir Edwin Arnold. "It is impossible," says Arnold, "to exaggerate the natural beauty of Ceylon. Belted with a double girdle of golden sands and waving palm-groves, the interior is one vast green garden of nature, deliciously disposed into plain and highland, valley and peak, where almost everything grows known to the tropical world, under a sky glowing with an equitorial sun, yet tempered by the cool sea-winds. Colombo itself, outside the actual town, is a perfect labyrinth of shady bowers and flowery streams and lakes. For miles and miles you drive about under arbours of feathery bamboos, broad-leaved bread-fruit trees, talipot and areca palms, cocoa-nut groves, and stretches of rice-field, sugar-cane and cinnamon, amid which at night the fire-flies dart about in glittering clusters. The lowest hut is embosomed in palm-fronds and the bright crimson blossoms of the hibiscus; while wherever intelligent cultivation aids the prolific force of nature, there is enough in the profusion of nutmegs and allspice, of the india-rubbers and cinchonas, of cannas, dracænas, crotons, and other wonders of the Singalese flora, to give an endless and delighted study to the lover of nature."

It should be recalled at this point that this was the second of our visits to Ceylon; and although on the first visit the preceding November no public addresses had been arranged for, we had been on this very account much more at liberty to study some of the most interesting and conspicuous of the native characteristics and customs. We were also at that time particularly fortunate in our host, Mr. Moscrop, who had been for a long time in Ceylon, in a position to discover the secrets of the native superstitious beliefs and practices much more authentically than was possible for the average long-time resident among them.

The missionary hymn already referred to passes quickly on from the recognition in the gross, so to say, of the pleasing aspects of this part of the world, to the declaration, "and only *man* is vile." I was surprised, then, to learn that fully one-third of the 150,000 inhabitants of the City of Colombo are Christians, more than half of this number, about 80,000 being Roman Catholics. But devil-worship is still very common and persistent all over Ceylon; not only among the aboriginal natives but also among the Tamils and Singhalese of the better classes, some of the latter relapsing into it even after they have become professing Christians. My host narrated in detail three instances among the larger number which had come under his personal observation.

In one case a Christian girl, who was the daughter of a native pastor and whose grandfather even had been a Christian, at the end of about a year of married life became impressed with the belief that

ONE VAST GREEN GARDEN OF NATURE

she was losing the affection of her husband. Instead of seeking advice from her own pastor, she secretly consulted with a devil-priest and employed him to exorcise the evil spirit which was exerting this alienating influence. With great show of difficulty and of the expense of such shepherding of his flock, the priest procured a skull which purported to be that of a first-born child also of a first-born, for three or four generations back. This skull he ordered to be placed for several successive nights in the crotch of a "demon-tree," in order to propitiate the demon who inhabited it. Afterward, the skull was to be burned under the place where the woman cooked her husband's rice; and as she stirred the rice certain incantations were to be repeated. The woman was discovered and disciplined for her relapse—poor perplexed soul!—into heathenish heresy, but—I am glad to report—much more mildly than the most zealous among the native brethren and sisters of the church thought appropriate.

In the second case, a girl had been having convulsions that were supposed to be caused by a demon which had taken possession of her. In this form of belief in demon-possession we meet everywhere one of the most ancient and terrifying and cruel of superstitions. A devil-priest was summoned and arrived with his outfit of acolytes and tom-toms. While the girl was lying in a convulsion on the verandah, the priest produced a cock to whose leg he tied one end of a string, and then tied the other end to the leg of the girl. Then began the furious beating of tom-toms and the dancing of the priest, until he had worked himself into a condition of frenzy. Suddenly he drew a knife and struck off the head of the cock and then cut the end of the string tied to the girl's leg. The priest declared that the demon had entered along the string into the body of the cock and had then gone off into the air at the instant when the head of the cock was struck from its body. He then departed after declaring that the girl was cured, taking the bird with him. It was not known whether the girl was permanently improved by the treatment she received; but it was authentically reported that the devil-priest had the rooster for dinner next day. Surely he ran an awful risk of assimilating some remnant of the demon.

In the third instance, the girl believed herself possessed of a devil, and had certainly been acting up to her belief. She had been behaving like one "all possessed." When Mr. Moscrop saw her, her hair was dishevelled and her countenance dark and fierce, with an expression fitly described as demoniacal. The priestly therapeutics began a wild dance to the beating of tom-toms, the girl dancing in exact imitation of the priest. It was ordered that this performance should be kept up for a full hour; but at the end of a half hour the priest himself was so much used-up that he was evidently anxious to bring his labors at healing to a speedy end. He asked Mr. Moscrop for the time, which was given to him as forty-five minutes by a watch one-quarter of an hour fast. Five minutes later, the priest inquired whether the time was not yet at an end; for the dance had been growing wilder and both participants in it seemed near the point of utter exhaustion. On being told that it was time for the ceremony to end, the dancing ceased, the girl fell back in a swoon, and the priest departed declaring that the demon would never again trouble her. Since it was so much trouble to get rid of the devil in this case, we can the more readily believe that his chance of getting a new grip upon the same sufferer was at least considerably lessened from that time onward.

By a study of articles written by a native savant and published in the Ceylon Branch of the Royal Asiatic Society's Journal, I learned some very interesting facts regarding the religious condition of the natives of the island. The natives of the lower orders seem to care very little about Buddhism, although it is the religion they profess; in most cases of real difficulty they do not freely resort to it or to its priests. Instead of Buddhism, the devil-worship of their ancestors for untold generations is the underlying, permanent, and practically efficient religion of the great multitude of the lower orders of the Singhalese.

The Singhalese believe that the demons they worship are of two kinds, bad and good. The *Taksayo*, or demons proper, are the cause of all the ills that flesh is heir to. But then there are the *Dewivos*, or *Dewatawos*, who are inferior gods not necessarily malignant but easily offended, when they become revengeful towards those who have displeased them. Each of these two classes of demons has its priests; but the worship of neither class flourishes wholly by the practice of its priesthood. The priests of the "not-necessarily-malignant" demons are subdivided into four classes, according to the *delights* of the demons they serve: Some there are who delight in propitiatory offerings; some who delight in living beings; some who delight in music, dancing and similar ceremonials; and some who delight in death.

The demonology of the Singhalese is naïve but sufficiently elaborate. There is a kingdom of devils, vast and numerous, with a cruel monarch *Wessamony* at its head. He loves tortures. There is a government of viceroys, ministers, and subordinate chiefs. Prescribed ceremonials of a pandemoniacal character are in order every Saturday and Wednesday of each week. There is a regular system of government licenses, without which the demons cannot inflict diseases or receive offerings. But certain freebooting demons exist.

The number of demons is beyond all calculation; but some fifty or sixty are most prominent, a sort of chiefs of the community. Of all, the worst is one whose special department is *blood!* He is described as having a human body with an ape's face, and he rides on a bull of a deep blood-red color. Another of these arch-demons has the department of corpses under his charge; he is the "grave-yard" demon. He is 122 feet high, and has three eyes and four hands, and his skin is of a deep blood-red color! There are demons of wind, of bile, of phlegm, etc., etc. The air is full of them. And, indeed, if one believe in demonology at all, why should one limit the number even to the multitude comprised in the elaborate demonology of the Singhalese? Modern civilization so-called can add a vast host more to those enumerated in so naïve a system.

But what is further to be noticed as a most significant fact in the history of comparative religions is this: Buddhism in Ceylon has not only tolerated but has incorporated into itself a considerable part of the native demonology. At least four-fifths, and perhaps nine-tenths, of the Buddhist temples resorted to by the common people have a central shrine dedicated to Buddha; but on one side, a shrine dedicated to some Hindu god (usually Vishnu); and, on the other side, a shrine dedicated to some devil (usually Pattini, the small-pox goddess). A Buddhistic work of great authority, as a matter of discipline for the monks, admonishes them not to throw stones or sticks or even to swing their arms when walking, lest they may strike some demon of the air and injure and anger him.

Belief in "demon trees" is almost universal among the natives of Ceylon. Even in the city limits of Colombo there are several such trees to be seen by the observing pedestrian. Thieves "conscientiously" avoid them. No non-Christian native would venture under or near one at night. Probably only the more emancipated Christians could avoid an involuntary shudder at their proximity. At any rate they are fain to turn aside or hurry by; unless the tree can be used as an asylum against the intending robber. Among the trees especially given over to demons are the *Ficus altissima*, the Cassia fistula, and the Beli tree. No one dares to cut down such a tree when full-grown; but they are carefully destroyed in the gardens before they are large enough for a demon to occupy.

The belief in demon-children is the most cruel of this class of superstitions: the belief still exists, however, and is widely prevalent; and there is reason to think that in the remoter country places the Government has never succeeded in completely suppressing the practices connected with it. Scarcely twenty years before the time of our visit, a child born with a profusion of hair an inch long, with teeth already cut, and with ill-proportioned features, was pronounced to be a "demon-child." Accordingly, its brains were beaten out with a club by the grandfather of the child. Under the watch of the present government, the facts in the remoter villages are difficult to ascertain; but infanticide on this ground is probably not so very infrequent up to the present time. As to the older native custom one may read in Robert Knox's strange book called "Historical Narration." There we are told: "As soon as the Child is born the Father or some Friend apply themselves to an *Astrologer* to enquire whether the Child be born in a *prosperous planet*, and a *good* hour or an *evil*. If it be found to be an *evil*, they presently destroy it, either by starving it, let it lie and die, or by drowning it, putting its head into a Vessel of water, or by burying it alive, or else by giving it to some body of the same degree with themselves . . . for they say the child will be unhappy to the parents and to none else. We have asked them why they will deal so with the poor Infants that come out of their bowels? They will indeed have a kind of regret and trouble at it. But they say withal, *Why should I bring up a Devil in my House?*"

Belief in astrology is nearly if not quite universal among the Singhalese,—as, indeed it is among all peoples of similar stages of scientific culture. Just before our arrival on the former visit to Ceylon there had been the greatest excitement in connection with the November shower of meteors. An Austrian astrologer of great repute was bruited abroad as having predicted that the world was surely coming to an end. The Buddhist inhabitants of the villages surrounding Colombo seemed to fear most this impending calamity; and the more so, since a Brahman who was supposed to have been favored with a vision while resting on a rock near the *Dampool Wihare,* was wandering about and distributing predictions of the arrival on the thirteenth of that month, of a demon that "was to cause the death of anyone who spoke in answer to his knocks on the doors." Even up to the time of our arrival the priests were kept busy saying *Pirit* and *Bana* in the temples, as well as at the residences of the more wealthy members of their flocks. Several begging friars were also parading the streets of the city; and almsgiving was carried on to an unexampled extent.

But there were pleasanter things to see and read about than those which have just been described, and some of them no less curious and interesting. No sooner had our ship come to anchor than its rigging and its rails were covered with swarms of beautiful butterflies; and, after we had landed, we saw other swarms flying along the shore of the sea. The region from which they come, annually and at this time of the year, is not well known; but the peculiar thing about their flight was said to be that they always fly against and never with the strong monsoon. The natives explain the phenomenon with the charming conceit that the butterflies are making their annual visit to the tomb of Buddha.

The same *corvus impudens* with which we made such intimate acquaintance in Madras is equally in evidence in Colombo. The crows congregate in a neighboring island which is named after them, at night; but during the day they swarm into and forage the city. They are credited with distributing its districts among themselves, the same birds reappearing at the same spots day after day and not allowing any visits from intruders.

The street scenes of Colombo have in only somewhat diminished degree the same charming variety of picturesquely colored and decorated animal and human forms. The bullocks which draw the carts are branded,—many in strangely fantastic and some of them in rather artistic fashion over a large portion of the entire hide. Different styles and colors of clothing and of head-dress—the Tamils wear turbans, the Singhalese go bare-headed, but wear conspicuous and curiously carved combs—give an air of thronged gaiety to all the principal thoroughfares, or dot the thickly shaded lanes along which are the huts of the poor, and the extensive compounds of the wealthy.

On the evening of the day of our arrival (Sunday) in Colombo, homeward-bound, I spoke in the church of the Wesleyan Methodists on the "Essentials of Christianity." The audience was fair in numbers, but apparently of not the same intellectual quality as most of the Indian audiences. After the address a communion-service was held, in the very impressive form of the Wesleyan Methodists, which I had never seen before. On the way back we had an illustration of the fashion in which the common soldier of the dominant foreign race is quite too apt to misbehave in his relations to the natives of the race he is so sure to regard as quite inferior. The driver of our garry was proceding along the street-car track at a fair but not extravagant pace, and two English "Tommies" were walking in front of his vehicle and in the same direction. The driver had made several attempts to attract their attention but without success. He was at last compelled to pull in his horse with a shout when its head was nearly over the shoulder of one of the soldiers. At this the Tommy turned and struck the poor brute a cruel blow in the face with the butt-end of his cane. We barely escaped being spilled by the roadside in a runaway; and when the horse was brought under control, the harness was so damaged as to be quite useless for draught purposes. We had to walk a mile or two before we could secure jinrickshas, and reached the compound of our host late and exhausted. The indignation passed, and the exhaustion was soon cured; but the memory of the walk in the moonlight by the sea on the Galle Face road will, in the wealth of charm which it affords, not soon pass nor be exhausted.

That same night we had our last and most startling, but in its issue entirely harmless and rather amusing, personal experience with the ways of the varied and ubiquitous reptile species in this quarter of the world. I was awakened by a curious noise of periodic thumping, as though between crawls; and since we had noticed before retiring that the French windows of our large bedroom opened upon a verandah with steps to the ground well adapted for climbing by snakes, I began at once to suspect a cobra of attempting to hitch himself across the floor of the room. I therefore cried out a sharp warning to the other occupant of the room, who was fast asleep in a bed a dozen feet from my own: "Wake up, don't step out of bed, but light your candle quickly." Light procured, feeble though it was, the nature of the disturbance to our slumbers was readily apparent. For each successive thump was followed by a billowing motion in the canvas-ceiling over our heads and by the squealing of a terrified rat, the cessation of which soon showed that the rat-snake had done well and thoroughly the very task for which he had some years before, when much smaller, been shut in between the ceiling and the roof of the bungalow.

Our last days in Ceylon were made memorable by one of the most delightful of excursions, entirely easy to be taken, anywhere upon the face of the habitable earth. This was the excursion to Kandy, headquarters of Buddhism in Ceylon, and indeed of

Southern Buddhism generally. The first mention of Kandy as a city is at the beginning of the 14th century, when a temple was built there, to contain one of Buddha's many mouthsful of teeth, and other relics of the same master's religion. From this beginning it grew into the site for residences of the different branches of the royal family and the seat of the Buddhistic hierarchical institutions. It was afterwards made the political capital of the island,—an eminence greatly to its misfortune, for it is usually disastrous to mix religion with too much politics. Kandy was so often burned in the wars between the Portuguese and the Dutch that scarcely any of the ancient buildings besides the temples and the royal residence were standing when the English took possession of it in 1815.

We rose at 5:30, had *chota hazri* at 6:15 and took the train at 7:10 from the terminal station of the railway to Kandy. The first two hours of the journey are rather monotonous for those already accustomed to tropical scenery; but to us who had not yet been surfeited with it, all was very interesting and beautiful. The jungle, so different from that of India; the varying hues of the paddy-fields; the chiaro-scuro of the bamboo-groves, always the most successful of nature's attempts at this style of delicate beauty; the stately water-buffalos, with their fine brown hides made lustrous by the warm sunshine, either plowing or standing knee-deep tethered in the parti-colored grasses; the gaily clad natives just glimpsed down the well-kept red-rock roads, or lying lazily chattering around the doors of their brown-thatched huts,—these and other charming sights prevented all sense of weariness or ennui, although the day was very hot. After we had gone into the refreshment-car for breakfast, and had begun the ascent to Kandy, the views from the car-windows became more varied with near valleys and distant mountains, rocks of either morphological or historical interest ("Bible Rock," "Castle Rock," and the rock down which the old monarchs of Kandy used to hurl their captives), and picturesque woods nearer by.

We left the train at Paradeniya, and after a hurried visit to the tea-factory near by, spent an hour or two walking and driving through the Royal Botanic Gardens, justly celebrated as the best of all places to study tropical vegetation. Such magnificence of verdure it is difficult to picture in dreamland and quite impossible to describe effectively in words. The Gardens cover about 150 acres and are encircled on three sides by a royal river. Among the most curious of its exotics is the wonderful *Coco de Mer*, the fruit of which has a double and sometimes triple formation, and is many times as large as the ordinary cocoa-nut, and sometimes weighs 40 or even 50 pounds. At one time great medicinal value was ascribed to it; and it is said that the

Emperor Rudolph II offered 4000 florins for a single specimen. If there is truth in what a visiting German scientist said for publication but perhaps facetiously, that there is a poisonous snake hanging from some limb of every tree in the Gardens, we saw no evidence of it; though there is not the least doubt that poisonous tree-snakes are particularly plentiful in the Royal Botanic Gardens near Kandy.

From the Gardens, by a road every hut along which, as well as every more pretentious dwelling, is embowered in a garden of cocoa-nut palms, bread-fruit trees, coffee-trees, and brilliant tropical shrubs of varieties strange to northern eyes, we drove to the City of Kandy. Its site is nearly 1700 feet above the sea-level, on the banks of a small lake and surrounded on all sides by picturesque hills. A road called "Lady Horton's Walk" winds around one of these hills; and on one of its almost precipitous sides, from the carriage one looks deep down into a valley through which rolls a beautiful river. In a park at its foot is the Governor's pavilion, a building of most attractive architecture. The whole place is a perfect paradise of the Oriental tropical kind. It is an almost cruel fate for travellers who have come so far to have only a few hours rather than as many weeks to admire and enjoy this center of southern Buddhism.

After driving around the artificial lake which the cruel Raja Singh constructed, we visited the temple on its shores—known as the "Temple of the Tooth"—and its celebrated Library of palm-leaf manuscripts. It was one of these, alleged to be most ancient, which I had some months before been permitted to handle as a special privilege in the Sanskrit College in Calcutta. It is claimed that the "sacred tooth" was brought to Ceylon a short time before the arrival of Fa Hian in 311 A.D., in charge of the Princess Kalinga who concealed it in the folds of her hair. Since that time it has been carried by forced seizure back to India, recovered, hidden for a long period, discovered by the Portuguese and taken off to Goa where it was burned by the archbishop in the presence of the Portuguese Viceroy and his court. Another tooth, which is supposed to be a facsimile of the original, has been substituted; but it is a piece of discolored ivory about two inches long and little less than an inch wide, and resembles the tooth of some animal (a crocodile?) rather than a human being. Its enshrinement, however, is worthy of the divine Buddha; for the disreputable pretender rests on a lotus flower of pure gold, under seven concentric metal shrines that are adorned with jewels in increasing richness as they diminish in size.

The Library at Kandy is exceedingly rich in Buddhist scriptures in the Pali language, many of which are most beautifully bound—if one can call it "binding"—in illuminated wooden or repouseé silver covers. On entering the Library a plate was at once thrust under my nose and the rupee lying upon it was a not altogether delicate hint that the contribution expected was to be a coin of not inferior value. When the hint was repeated, however, it was finally met with a refusal: "No. I have already given enough, and I am too poor to give more." I regretted afterward that I had not told them: "Of all the many Buddhist temples I have ever visited you have much the meanest beggars; you are no better than Hindus in your shameless begging."

On the train down to Colombo, in spite of the wearisome heat, we enjoyed the charming views not a whit less, but if possible even more, than when we had first seen them. We reached dinner and bed, well spent indeed, but never better satisfied with a day's excursion than that which took us to and from the sacred center of Southern Buddhism (not of the *Mahā-Vagga*, or so-called "Greater Vehicle" to be sure), with its collection of the *Ti-Pitika* or "The Three Baskets" or Testaments, of the canon of Buddhistic scriptures in the Pali language, now accounted "to furnish the most authoritative information of the Buddha and his doctrine that we have." We had indeed only seen the jeweled covers of a few of these scriptures; but we could henceforth collect, as occasion required, some of the jewels of thought which they conveyed, by reference to English translations, with quickened memories and more enlightened interest.

"Even as a man hemmed in by foes,
Seeking a certain safe escape,
And nathless seeking not to flee,
Might not the blameless pathway chide;

"So, when my passions hem me in,
And yet a way to bliss exists,
Should I not seek to follow it,
That way of bliss I might not chide."

The "lecturing campaign," if so it may be called, which had begun in Japan and which had included considerably more than one-hundred addresses on topics of educational, philosophical, and religious interest, came to a close with an address on "Immortality in the Light of Modern Science," the evening of the day before we left Ceylon. The audience was larger, and seemed more intellectually keen and more deeply interested than had the other audiences which I addressed in Colombo. A bullock-cart and jinrickshas brought us to the jetty, from which the conveyance to the ship "Derbyshire" in the offing was smooth and quick, and so in most marked contrast with the rough and dangerous passage on board the "Chusan," when a tropical thunder-storm and its hurricane of wind had only partially subsided, in November of the preceding year.

For the last time we were entertained with the spectacle of a great ship getting ready to sail from one of the large cities of the tropics along this thronged line of ocean traffic. The scene aboard and around the ship had its customary varied and lively aspect. Boys were diving for small coins which they had coaxed the passengers standing by the rail to throw into the water; other boys were climbing the ship's side or dancing on their small rafts, whacking their naked sides to keep the rag-time of the ditties they were singing; venders of cheap jewelry and other jimcracks were trying to coax the passengers away from the rail, to inspect their wares and perchance yield to their importunities and their vociferous lying; boats were bringing loads of passengers aboard or conveying away the friends who had said their last tearful or laughing farewells; and swarms of dark-skinned coolies were loading on the last of a cargo which, for variety and strangeness of its commodities, can be matched nowhere outside of tropical waters. For us it was a mingling of sadness and pleasure to have to say: "Good-bye, vastly interesting and mysterious India; good-bye exquisitely charming but as yet scarcely half-redeemed Ceylon."

The "Derbyshire" sailed promptly from the offing at Colombo at six o'clock in the afternoon of the eighth of March, 1900; the entire voyage of twelve days to Ismailiya, which had been dreaded so much on account of the predicted terrific heat, really proved most comfortable, refreshing and restful. After the first few hours the thermometer in our cabin was never much, if any, above eighty; and when we reached the Red Sea, instead of rising, as it usually does at that time of the year, we were favored with a strong cool breeze from the North-east. Indeed, many of the passengers began to develop influenzas, fevers, and neuralgias, due to a sudden drop of nearly thirty degrees in the temperature.

The passenger fare, which was chiefly from Burmah, afforded few companions; but to sit and read in the open air, in summer clothing, and at times to rest the eyes by watching the sailors, or the rush of the smooth waters, or the flight of the birds, was pastime enough for those who had just come from a surfeit of other more exacting activities of an intellectual and social kind.

By listening to the conversation of a "burgher" who had been a magistrate in Ceylon, I heard repeated the customary denunciations of all the native races of all that part of the world. In his opinion, based upon thirty years of experience with them, the Singhalese were the most degraded and dishonest race upon the face of the earth. The Singhalese misses, whose fathers had got a little property,—apeing aristocratic foreign manners—insisted on having a coolie-girl to carry their prayer-books to church for them! The native barristers, police and other officers, were almost universally corrupt. But, on being questioned, my informant admitted that the English Government officers had not always been shining examples of unimpeachable virtue; and he especially instanced one of them, whose name is known all over the world as a writer on Buddhism, as having habitually received presents from the head-men of the villages, and as having been dismissed from the service for having lied about the bribery when he was accused of it. He also admitted that the Singhalese were probably no worse than the native races of Bengal and of Burmah; while, on the other hand, a gentleman who had lived a long time in Burmah gave a much more favorable account of both priests and people in that British Province. On this whole matter,—now so increasingly important on account of our growing and tightening relations with Oriental peoples of various races and degrees of civilization or barbarism—it is my experience that men are everywhere essentially alike; although the ways of showing the good or the bad disposition and intent vary wonderfully. These ways of expressing goodness and badness you have to know before you can judge the real man fairly.

At length we were inside the Gulf of Suez, with the land visible on either side. The shores of Arabia and of Egypt, even when wholly barren, are exceedingly picturesque. How strange to think that centuries ago in time, but only a few miles distant in space, Mosaism and Muhammadanism originated; and separated by a narrow strip of water and of land, the monarchies of ancient Egypt rose and fell.

And now, just before the bugle blew for dinner

we came to anchor off Suez at the entrance to the Canal. It was a fairy-like scene which was to be enjoyed as we lay there for more than two hours passing quarantine and complying with the other regulations necessary to admit us through the Canal. When, about ten o'clock, the full moonlight made faint the rows of red and green buoys on either side of the Canal, the view became even more weird, soft and enchanting. At three o'clock of that moonlit night the ship turned into the basin opposite the customhouse at Ismailiya, and without quite stopping took aboard the dozen of new passengers waiting on the harbor launch. Then, after letting our luggage into the same launch, careful hands lowered us enough to enable us to jump into the arms of the sailor standing in the ship's shadow below. The gong rang "Speed ahead," and the "Derbyshire" moved into the further moonlight and was soon lost to sight. Thus it cut the last link that bound our senses to the winter spent in India.

After I had given the Turk, who was even at this uncanny hour seated "at the receipt of customs," word of honor that we had nothing which the law did not permit in the various pieces of luggage, they were left in the customs-house, and their owner went to join his wife in the Inn "Victoria" across the way, for the few hours until the morning train should start for Cairo.

Here ends the story briefly told of how in somewhat more than a half-year of time we had come from the *Far* East to the *Near* East, gathering much information, making many friends, and—we faintly hoped—distributing some bits of good influence, by the way. We had seen numerous kinds of peoples and types of civilization;—their ways of transacting business and of social intercourse, their varying costumes and strange customs, their manner of welcoming the new-born babe into the world, of disciplining or neglecting him, of feasting and of mourning, of marrying their youth and burying their dead; in a word, what they thought of life and how they took it all, so far as could be judged from their most ordinary or more secret conventions, and their prevalent forms of expressing the heart's emotions in words and conduct. Best of all of our privileges, and on the whole profitable, was the rare opportunity which had been so freely and painstakingly provided to give us some intimate acquaintance with the five greatest of religions, of Confucianism, Buddhism, Hinduism, Muhammadanism, and Christianity—their beliefs, ceremonial, and precepts for the regulation of the practical life. In a word, we had come from the Land of the Rising Sun, stopping longest under the high lights and amidst the deep shadows of India, to finish all our observations and experiences by going to slumber under the mysterious moonlight that shone on the Deserts of Arabia and the Valley of the Nile.

INDEX